Fungarium

LIBRARY
GUILD OF
RANCHO
SANTA FE

For my mum, Viv
KS
To the next generation of mycologists!
EG

Text copyright © 2019 by the Board of Trustees of the Royal Botanic Gardens, Kew
Illustrations copyright © 2019 by Katie Scott

Text by:
The Tree of Life, Ester Gaya; Gallery 1: What Is a Fungus?, David L. Hawksworth and Ester Gaya; Sexual Reproduction, David L. Hawksworth and Ester Gaya; Asexual Reproduction, David L. Hawksworth and Ester Gaya; Spores, David L. Hawksworth and Ester Gaya; Growth, David L. Hawksworth and Ester Gaya; Ecosystem: Mountains, Laura M. Suz and Kare Liimatainen

Gallery 2: Cup Fungi, Lee Davies; Mushrooms and Toadstools, Kare Liimatainen; Bracket Fungi, Laura M. Suz; Gasteromycetes, Lee Davies; Foliicolous Fungi, Ester Gaya; Ecosystem: Temperate Forests, Laura M. Suz

Gallery 3: Mycorrhizas, Laura M. Suz; Mycorrhizal Networks, Laura M. Suz; Lichens, Ester Gaya; Entomogenous Fungi, Pepijn W. Kooij; Ants and Termites, Pepijn W. Kooij

Gallery 4: Early Mycologists, David L. Hawksworth and Ester Gaya; Plant Pathogens, Tom Prescott; Poisonous Fungi, Lee Davies; Edible Fungi, Kare Liimatainen; Wonder Drugs, Tom Prescott; Ecosystem: Tropical Forests, David L. Hawksworth and Ester Gaya

All rights reserved. No part of this book may be reproduced, transmitted, or stored in an information retrieval system in any form or by any means, graphic, electronic, or mechanical, including photocopying, taping, and recording, without prior written permission from the publisher.

First US edition 2021
First published by Big Picture Press, an imprint of Bonnier Books UK, 2019

Library of Congress Catalog Card Number pending
ISBN 978-1-5362-1709-4

20 21 22 23 24 25 WKT 10 9 8 7 6 5 4 3 2 1

Printed in Shenzhen, Guangdong, China

This book was typeset in Gill Sans and Mrs Green.
The illustrations were done in ink and colored digitally.

BIG PICTURE PRESS
an imprint of
Candlewick Press
99 Dover Street
Somerville, Massachusetts 02144

www.candlewick.com

Artwork not to scale

Fungarium

illustrated by KATIE SCOTT

written by DAVID L. HAWKSWORTH, LAURA M. SUZ, PEPIJN W. KOOIJ, KARE LIIMATAINEN, TOM PRESCOTT, LEE DAVIES, and ESTER GAYA

BPP

FUNGARIUM

Preface

Fungi are probably the least known and most misunderstood organisms on Earth. More closely related to animals than to plants, they are critical to the maintenance of our food supply, health, ecosystems, and global atmospheric chemistry. They also exhibit an amazing variety of adaptations and forms.

Fungi impinge on almost all aspects of our lives and are all around us; even as you read this, you are breathing in some microscopic fungal spores from the air. Life would not be as we know it without them. Forests and crops need them to flourish: without them, dead wood and leaves would never fully decay but would instead accumulate year after year. Cattle and sheep, along with other ruminant animals, need some fungi in their stomachs to break down the grass they eat. Stores would be without coffee, tea, chocolate, many cheeses, alcoholic drinks, biological detergents, soy sauce, vinegar, mushrooms, mushroom products, and more. Our lives would also be shorter without antibiotics and other pharmaceutical products made from fungi. On the downside, some fungi can grow on and in us, kill our crops and trees, spoil our food, invade our homes, or even poison us.

Yet we know barely 5 percent of the 2.2–3.8 million fungal species on Earth, and previously unknown fungi can be found almost anywhere—even in your own backyard. Species new to science are continually being discovered. Their vast extent has only come to light in the last few years from molecular studies. These studies have revealed that there are staggeringly huge numbers of species that have never even been seen and are known only from their DNA.

Professor David L. Hawksworth CBE
Royal Botanic Gardens, Kew, London, England

1
Entrance
Welcome to Fungarium 1
The Tree of Life 4

7
Gallery 1
Fungal Biology
What Is a Fungus? 8
Sexual Reproduction 10
Asexual Reproduction 12
Spores 14
Growth 16
Ecosystem: Mountains 18

21
Gallery 2
Fungal Diversity
Cup Fungi 22
Mushrooms and Toadstools 24
Bracket Fungi 26
Gasteromycetes 28
Foliicolous Fungi 30
Ecosystem: Temperate Forests 32

35
Gallery 3
Fungal Interactions
Mycorrhizas 36
Mycorrhizal Networks 38
Lichens 40
Entomogenous Fungi 42
Ants and Termites 44

47
Gallery 4
Fungi and Humans
Early Mycologists 48
Plant Pathogens 50
Poisonous Fungi 52
Edible Fungi 54
Wonder Drugs 56
Ecosystem: Tropical Forests 58

61
Library
Index 62
Curators 64
To Learn More 64

FUNGARIUM

Entrance

Welcome to Fungarium

Fungi are hardly mentioned in science classes; they remain a big unknown for many. We have put together a special museum so you can explore this mysterious kingdom. In these pages, you will see magnified microscopic fungi, get inside animals, climb mountains, and have a glimpse of the underground world inhabited by fungi.

Tour the galleries and learn why fungi are more related to animals than to plants. Discover how they evolved. Find out about their amazing variety of shapes and colors, some of them alien-like, almost monstrous, and disgustingly smelly, others incredibly beautiful. The illustrations in this book are not to scale because fungi vary so much in size. Some are microscopic while others are surprisingly large—one *Rigidoporus ulmarius* at Kew Gardens (pages 26–27) had a bracket with a circumference of around 16 feet/ 5 meters!

Have you ever heard about the "zombie fungi" that can take control of insect bodies? And the caterpillar fungi used in traditional Chinese medicine? Discover the most important lifesaving drugs that come from fungi; some have revolutionized human transplant surgery. Learn also about fungi that can be eaten and that represent some of the world's finest delicacies. But be cautious and remember that some of them may kill you. In addition, let *Fungarium* introduce you to the underground world of mycorrhizal networks, the key players in all terrestrial ecosystems.

As you travel through *Fungarium*, you will learn more about fungi's multiplicity of forms, adaptations, and habitats and about their importance to us and to the world we live in. We are sure you will become as enthralled, fascinated, and excited by fungi as we are.

Dr. Ester Gaya
Royal Botanic Gardens, Kew, London, England

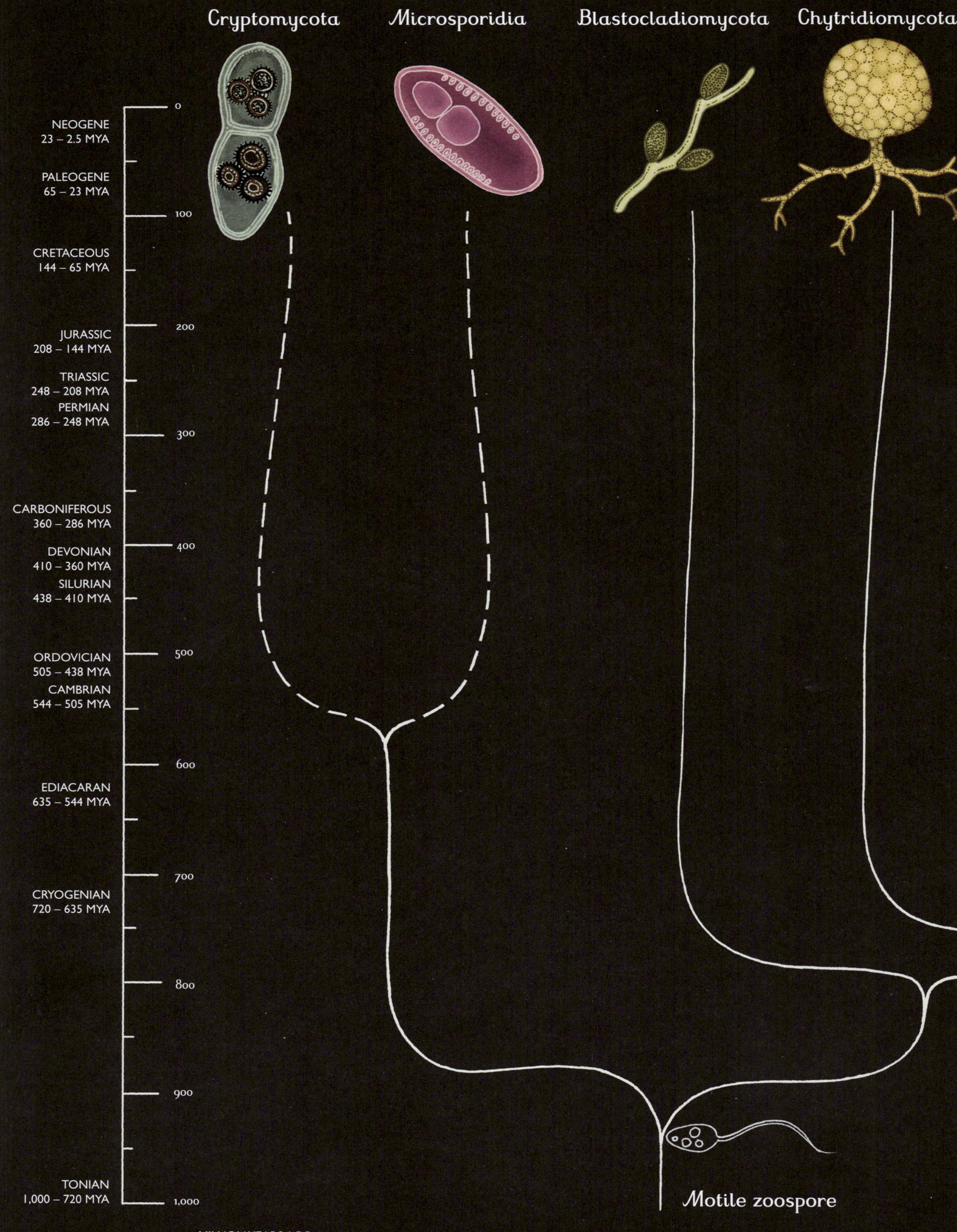

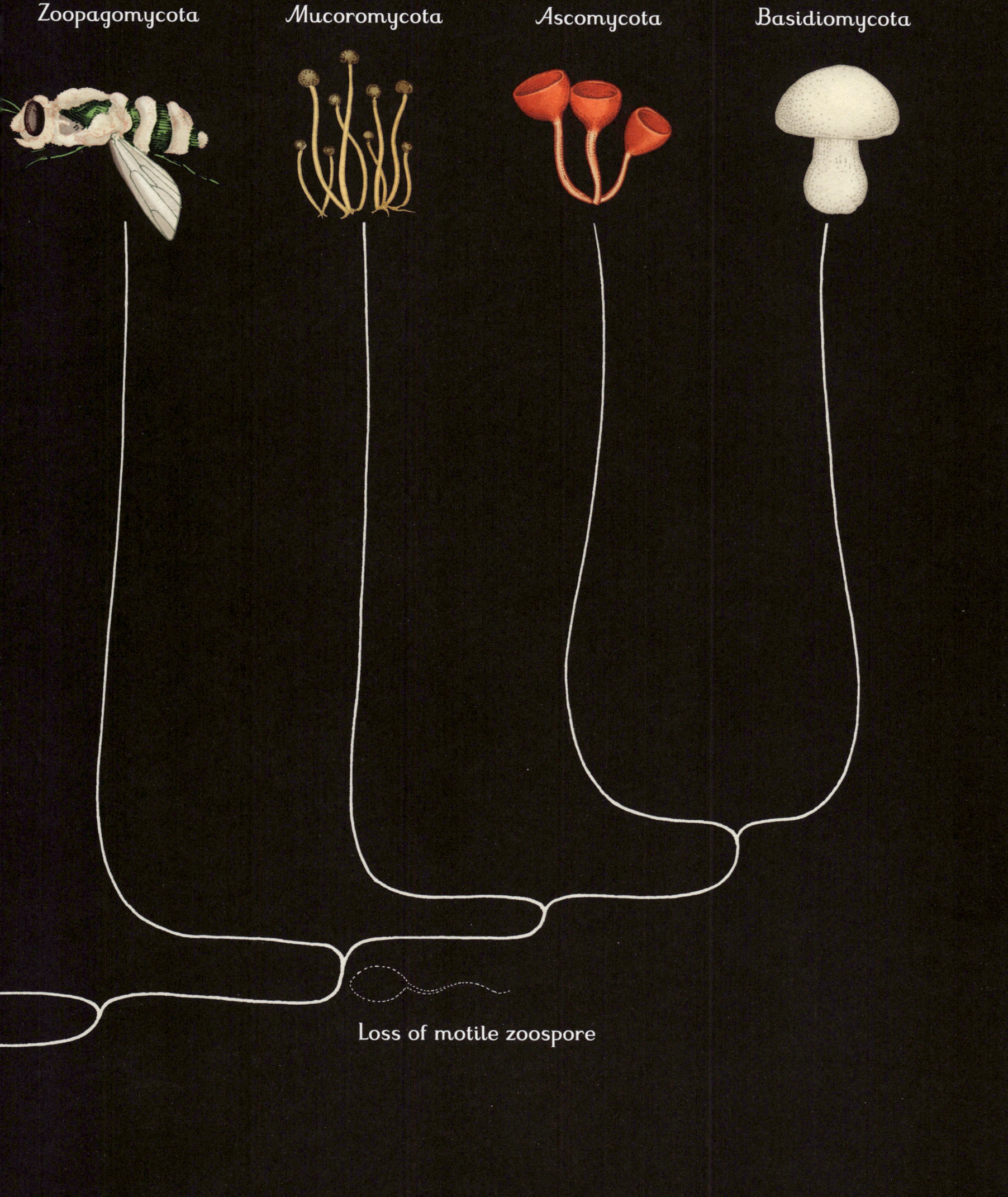

FUNGARIUM

The Tree of Life

All species on Earth are related and connected in a "tree of life." Reconstructing this tree allows us to tell the story of evolutionary history. What does the fungal tree of life look like?

It turns out that this is a difficult question to answer. Sometimes similar-looking fungi are not at all closely related, and even more problematically, a large proportion of species are still awaiting discovery, hidden underground, or within the cells of other organisms. Without an accurate idea of the diversity and relationships of the fungi species alive today, it is difficult to build an understanding of historical relationships of the kingdom Fungi.

Identifying similarities and differences in DNA is helping us to understand how the branches of the fungal tree fit together. This includes the discovery of new branches such as the Cryptomycota and Microsporidia, two early groups that were thought not to contain a substance called chitin, which is one of the key features of fungi. DNA and detailed microscopy studies have proved this wrong. Other groups, including downy mildews (Oomycota) and slime molds (Myxomycota), have been proven to not belong to the Fungi kingdom.

The earliest fungi are thought to have evolved around one billion years ago and to have been simple, single-celled organisms that lived in water. They reproduced using asexual spores called zoospores that were motile, meaning they were capable of movement. They propelled themselves with a whiplike structure called a flagellum. Modern-day Cryptomycota, Chytridiomycota, and Blastocladiomycota share some of these features.

The evolutionary transition from aquatic to land-dwelling fungi is estimated to have taken place around 700 million years ago. The first two groups to evolve in the new environment were the Zoopagomycota and Mucoromycota, which lacked motile spores. Zoopagomycota are almost exclusively pathogens, parasites, or commensals (organisms that live on or within animals and other fungi without harming them). In contrast, Mucoromycota form associations with plants.

Around 600–700 million years ago, two fungal groups known as Ascomycota and Basidiomycota evolved. These groups contain species that form highly complex spore-bearing structures. Together they contain the vast majority of known fungal species—around 140,000 in total. They also include the single-celled yeasts, which have arisen in multiple diverse lineages, and other microscopic fungi.

Research on the fungal tree continues, and there are still many questions arising from the ever-increasing rate at which species are being discovered. A whole new "invisible dimension of fungal diversity" in our soils, bodies, and waterways, the so-called dark taxa, is also being revealed. Mycologists are only starting to explore this unknown territory.

FUNGARIUM

Gallery 1

Fungal Biology

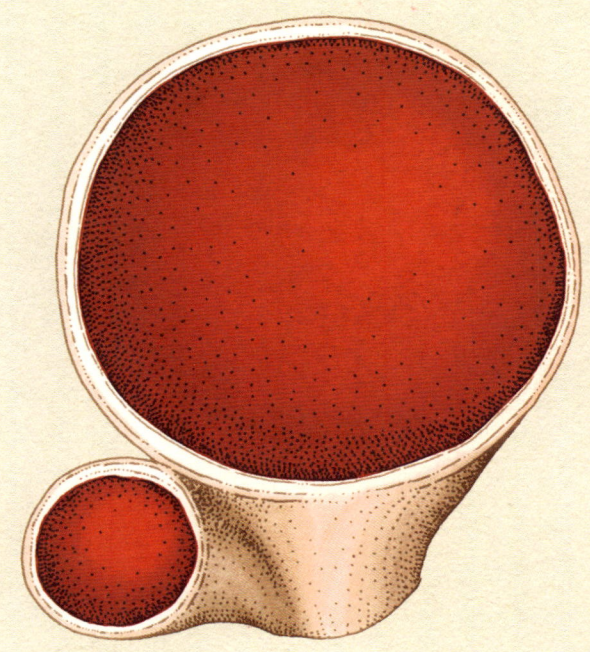

What Is a Fungus?
Sexual Reproduction
Asexual Reproduction
Spores
Growth
Ecosystem: Mountains

FUNGAL BIOLOGY

What Is a Fungus?

Fungi have a kingdom of their own, just as animals and plants do, but theirs is by far the least known. As new species are constantly being discovered, scientists think we have barely scratched the surface and that of the estimated 2.2 to 3.8 million species on Earth, fewer than 5 percent have been identified.

Historically, fungi were treated as plants and studied by botanists. They were included in the great catalog of plants, *Species Plantarum*, compiled by the naturalist Carl Linnaeus in 1753. That is why it often comes as a surprise to learn that fungi are more closely related to animals than they are to plants. Just like the outer skeletons of insects and crustaceans, fungal cell walls are made largely of chitin, a substance similar to the keratin of human hair and skin. Plant cell walls contain cellulose instead. Plants manufacture their own food from carbon dioxide in the air, light, and water through a process called photosynthesis. Like animals, fungi can't manufacture their nutrients. However, whereas animals ingest their food by engulfing or swallowing it, fungi secrete enzymes that dissolve food outside their bodies, then absorb the nutrients through their cell walls. Another obvious difference between animals and fungi is that animals move around to search for food, while fungi grow toward it.

There are at least eight phyla (major groups) of true fungi, although some researchers recognize up to eighteen or more! These phyla include Cryptomycota, Microsporidia, Blastocladiomycota, Chytridiomycota, Zoopagomycota, Mucoromycota, Ascomycota, and Basidiomycota. Some of the most ancient are single-celled and don't look at all like typical fungi. Most familiar fungi belong to Ascomycota and Basidiomycota. The species in these two groups produce filaments called septate hyphae and include mushrooms, yeasts, and fungi that associate with algae to form lichens.

Key to plate

1: **Rozella sp.**
(Cryptomycota)
Motile zoospore
This motile zoospore, with an appendage called a flagellum enabling it to swim, is reminiscent of spermatozoids and reminds us of our close connection to fungi.

2: **Rhizophydium planktonicum**
(Chytridiomycota)
This is an ancient fungus that lives mainly in water and soil. It is a parasite of a microscopic freshwater diatom, or single-celled alga, called *Asterionella*.

3: **Piromyces communis**
(Chytridiomycota)
Piromyces communis can be found in the digestive system of herbivores. It produces enzymes that help the animals digest fibers from plant cell walls. Chytrids are generally single-celled with delicate filaments called rhizoids that can penetrate host tissues.

4: **Berwaldia schaefernai**
(Microsporidia)
Spore (sporoblast)
Each spore is surrounded by a vesicle, or storage sac, composed of a thin outer membrane-like sheath and an inner layer of tubular structures. The external layer is made of proteins and chitin. Microsporidians are single-celled parasites of animals.

5: **Black bread mold**
(Mucoromycota)
Rhizopus stolonifer
Mucoromycota have more developed structures than earlier groups and form networks of filaments, but without the cell-delimiting walls usually found in Ascomycota and Basidiomycota.

6: **Caesar's mushroom**
(Basidiomycota)
Amanita caesarea
This familiar fungus (see also page 54) is in the phylum Basidiomycota. In basidiomycetes, spores form on microscopic cells known as basidia.

7: **Darwin's fungus**
(Ascomycota)
Cyttaria darwinii
This fungus belongs to a genus of highly evolved parasitic fungi that only grow on species of southern beech trees. In ascomycete species, spores are formed inside cells known as asci.

8: **Upright coral**
(Basidiomycota)
Ramaria stricta
This basidiomycete does not look like a typical mushroom. The sporing body has multiple slender and vertical parallel branches covered by spores.

9: **Cladia aggregata lichen**
(Ascomycota)
Around 98 percent of lichens belong to the phylum Ascomycota. *Cladia* presents a unique growth form with numerous perforations along upright extensions of the thallus (the body of the fungus).

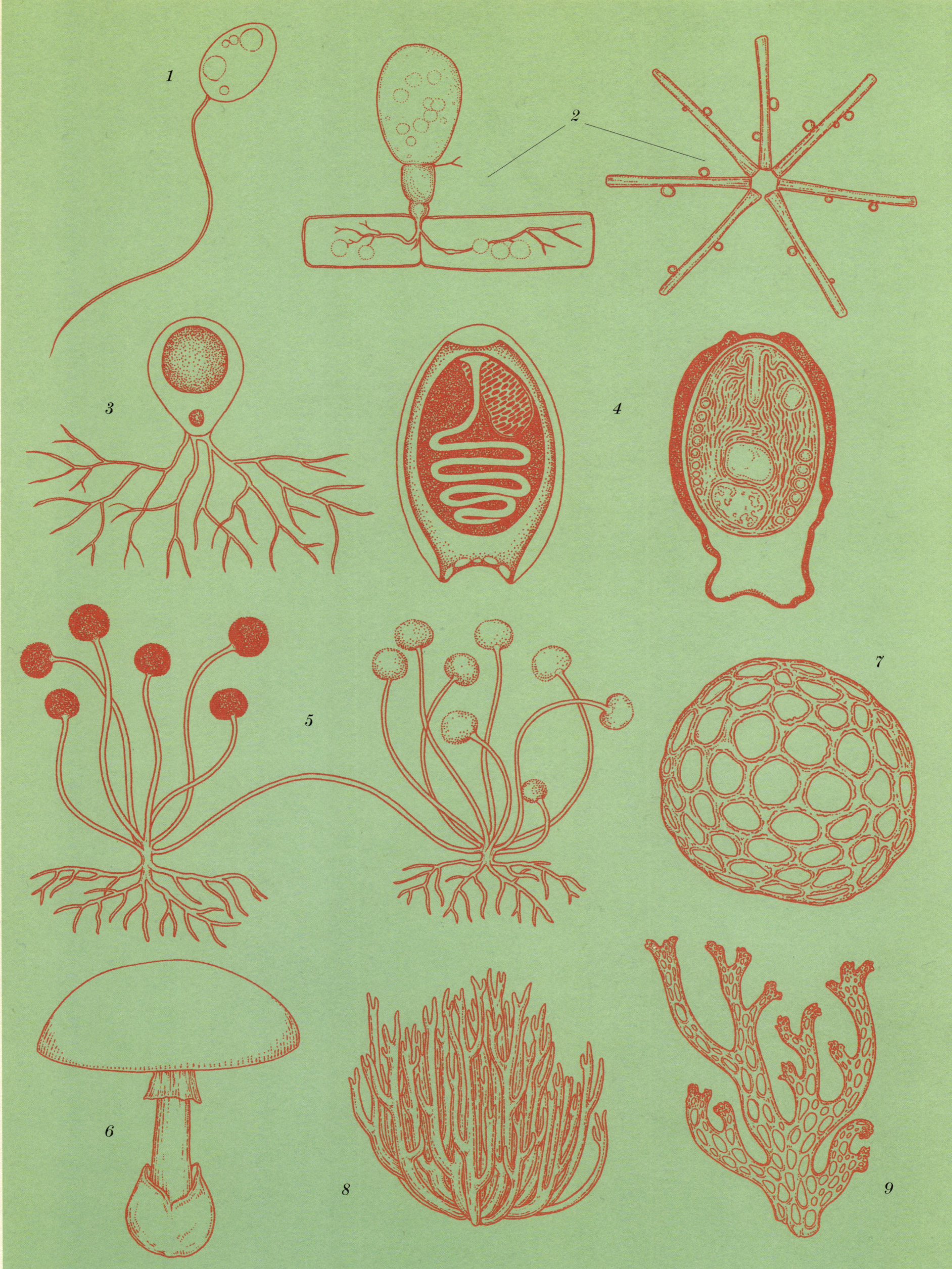

FUNGAL BIOLOGY

Sexual Reproduction

Fungi are very special in terms of reproductive abilities: many of them can reproduce both sexually and asexually. This is rare, and has caused great confusion in the past, as mycologists would often name each reproductive form as a distinct species. Even today, scientists may have to use DNA to identify reproductive pairs of the same fungus.

Sexual reproduction in fungi can only be seen with a microscope. When it occurs, two nuclei (the membrane-bound structures that contain the cell's genetic material), each with a single set of chromosomes (threadlike structures in which the DNA is packaged in the nucleus), must fuse together. It is a complex process that involves cell division and the exchange and rearrangement of genes. Living organisms, including fungi, do this because it ensures genetic diversity, fundamental to evolution and ultimately survival. The fusing nuclei can be from the same individual or from different individuals of the same species. Once nuclei are fused, they remain in special cells from which new spore-producing structures arise. The new spores will form new fungal colonies.

In the two largest groups of fungi, Ascomycota and Basidiomycota, the spore-producing cells are concealed within structures known as ascomata and basidiomata. In ascomycetes, spores (ascospores) are formed inside sacs called asci, from which they are released in an extraordinary number of ways: the ascus may disintegrate to form a spore mass or forcefully squirt its spores out like a water pistol. By contrast, in basidiomycetes, spores (basidiospores) are produced inside structures called basidia but develop externally on small point-like structures called sterigmata. In mushrooms, basidia form on gills below the caps, and spores are shot bullet-like by an ingeniously moving water droplet—generally just for the tiny distance needed to liberate them from the gills.

Key to plate

1: **Common field mushroom**
Agaricus campestris
(a) Development of a mushroom, one of many forms that sporing bodies in the phylum Basidiomycota can take. Once the cap opens, the veil breaks and the exposed gills release spores.
(b) Portion of an enlarged gill showing basidia and basidiospores on sterigmata.

2: ***Zygorhynchus* sp.**
(a) The process of hyphae coming together to form a zygosporangium
(b) Zygosporangium and zygospore formed
This fungus has a peculiar reproductive system. Two hyphae come together as sexual partners and are bridged by hyphal tubes that form thick-walled, resistant spores (zygospores) in structures called zygosporangia.

3: **Common jellyspot fungus**
Dacrymyces stillatus
This typically orange gelatinous fungus stands out for its basidia, which are fork-shaped and branched and produce sausage-shaped spores.

4: **Common rust fungus**
Phragmidium violaceum
This fungus has a complex life cycle with sexual and asexual stages and different types of spores. The stalked spore (teliospore) includes a row of four cells with two nuclei each. As the teliospore cells germinate, the nuclei fuse, and cell division will be followed by the rise of basidia.

5: **Candlestick or candle-snuff fungus**
Xylaria hypoxylon
As in most ascomycetes, the asci of this fungus contain eight spores. Here the spores have a germ slit (a thin area of the cell wall running the length of the spore). There is a huge range of ascus types; their structure and method of discharge vary according to their taxonomic group. In *Xylaria* there is an apical structure through which the spores are discharged.

6: **Dog lichen**
Peltigera canina
This lichen species produces asci with a special form of spore discharge. The ascus wall and its outer layer rupture, and the thick apical material of the inner layer expands to form a lip structure (the rostrum). After spore release, the inner layer returns to its place like an accordion.

Asexual Reproduction

Sexual reproduction in fungi can be a complicated and slow process, so many have developed alternative strategies for propagating themselves, establishing new colonies without sex. This is called asexual reproduction. Some fungi produce one or more kinds of asexual reproductive structures as well as sexual ones, while in others no sexual structures are known at all. The advantage of an asexual strategy is that it can produce massive numbers of genetically identical spores, which can rapidly grow on new sites.

Asexual spores are produced by simple cell division, and their nuclei have just one set of chromosomes. The most common type of asexual spores are conidia, which form from specialized cells in a mind-blowing number of ways. They can be produced directly from hypha-like structures called conidiophores, from hyphae fused together to form pin-like formations, from mounds in compact groups, or even inside a variety of structures called conidiomata from which they can be discharged through a pore or split. Conidia can form individually, in chains, or in ball-like clumps and can either be dry or produced in slimy droplets, depending on their method of dispersal.

There are other asexual ways fungi get around. Yeast cells, which are constantly dividing, can also function as conidia, and separated pieces of hyphae can be carried inadvertently by animals or inside plant tissues. In most cases, asexual spores do not travel as far as sexual spores, and only a small proportion end up being widely disseminated by air currents or wind. These are mainly species producing large numbers of small dry spores that often cause allergies.

Key to plate

1: Alternaria alternata
This is a plant pathogen that causes leaf spot in various plant species and can also cause respiratory infections in humans. Its conidiophores produce light-brown septate (with divisions) conidia, which form chains.

2: Coemansia erecta
Species of *Coemansia* are microscopic saprobes, meaning they get their nutrients from dead or decaying organic matter; they can be found in dung, soil, or other organic materials or on dead animals and insects.
(a) Their asexual structures, shown here, present elegant shapes.
(b) Here, the spore-bearing structures carry spores lined up, looking like a toothbrush.

3: Thielaviopsis basicola
This plant pathogen can cause devastating crop diseases, such as black rot or stem-end rot. It can have two types of asexual spores:
(a) simple translucent tube-shaped conidiophores with colorless spores or
(b) septate brown spores

4: Periconia byssoides
This saprobic species can be found on dead plants. It reproduces asexually and is not known to have a sexual stage. In reproduction it forms simple conidiophores that carry many rounded, minutely spiny brown conidia.
(a) general view of conidiophore
(b) magnified view of conidiophore

5: Lasiodiplodia theobromae
This plant pathogen lives on a wide variety of hosts. It usually causes rotting and dieback in many tropical crops after they have been harvested. Conidia in this species are initially translucent but become darkly colored.

6: Tetracladium sp.
Tetracladium species are known only from their asexual state, which includes special four-branched conidia like the one shown here. *Tetracladium* is aquatic, growing on plant litter in streams.

7: Parmelina pastillifera
Many lichens have the ability to reproduce both sexually and asexually, often simultaneously. The most common lichen structures in asexual reproduction are soralia and isidia, which are able to distribute algal and fungal partners together as single packages. Isidia, seen here, include an outer layer called a cortex that protects both partners, whereas soralia do not have a cortex.

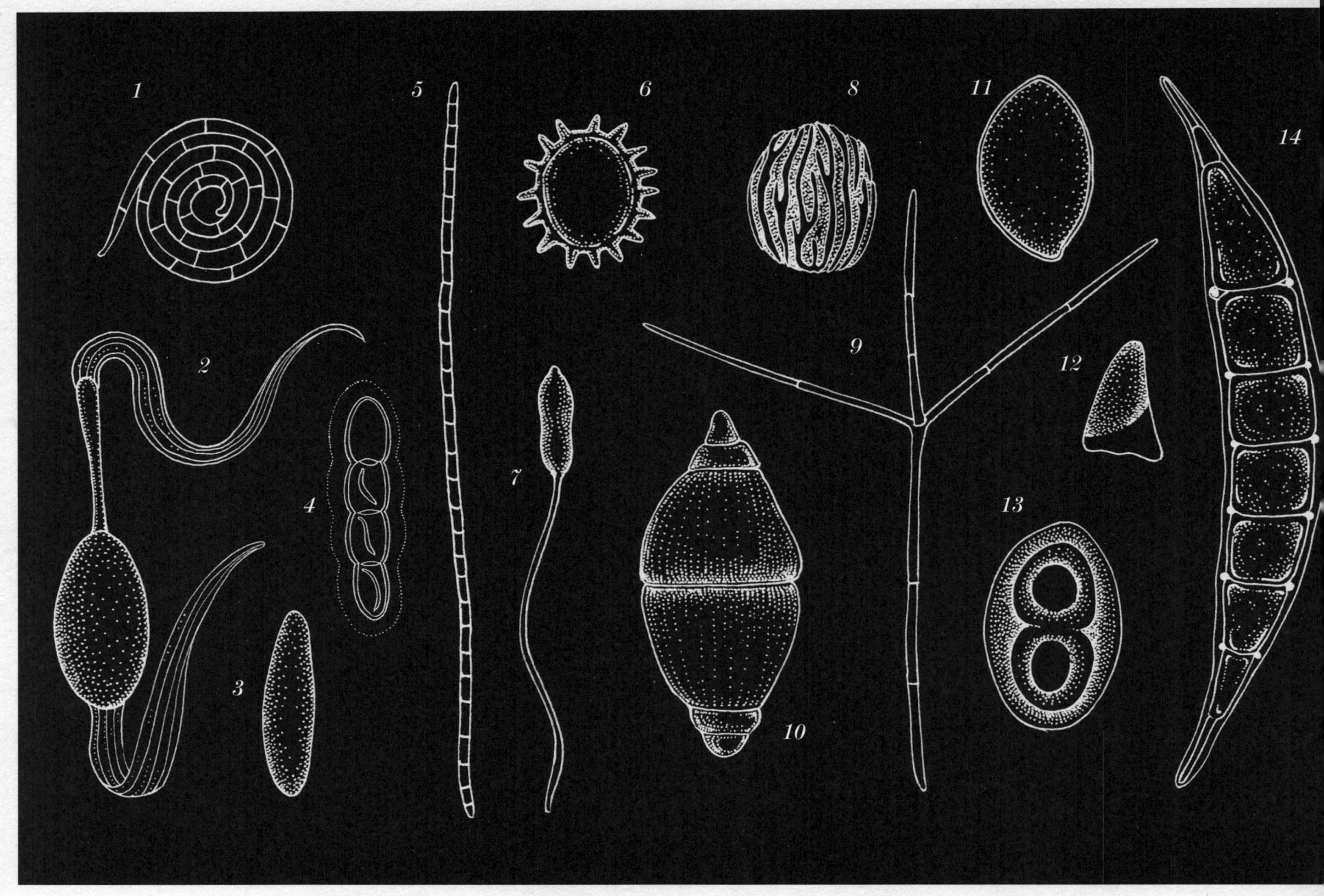

FUNGAL BIOLOGY

Spores

Spores are reproductive cells produced by fungi. The diversity of fungal spores, both sexual and asexual, is truly amazing, from single cells of just a couple of micrometers (a unit of measurement equal to one-thousandth of a millimeter, abbreviated as μm) to huge ones visible even with the unaided eye. The incredible myriad of shapes found in spores includes minute spheres, enormous ellipsoid structures, and delicate threads or coils, some branched, others star-like. Colors vary from transparent to white, pink, or various shades of brown to black; sometimes separate cells within a spore have different pigments.

Spore walls can have various layers, and the surfaces can feature all kinds of textures and ornaments, including pores or slits through which they germinate or scars produced when they are formed. Some have outer coatings, including jellylike sheaths or appendages ranging from almost invisible whiplike threads to complex gelatinous heads and tails. Beneath the outer layers, many have internal walls making several compartments, which can germinate independently.

The form of the spores, and whether they are dry or slimy, depends on their method of dispersal. Some stick together to form massive projectiles, which when ejected can

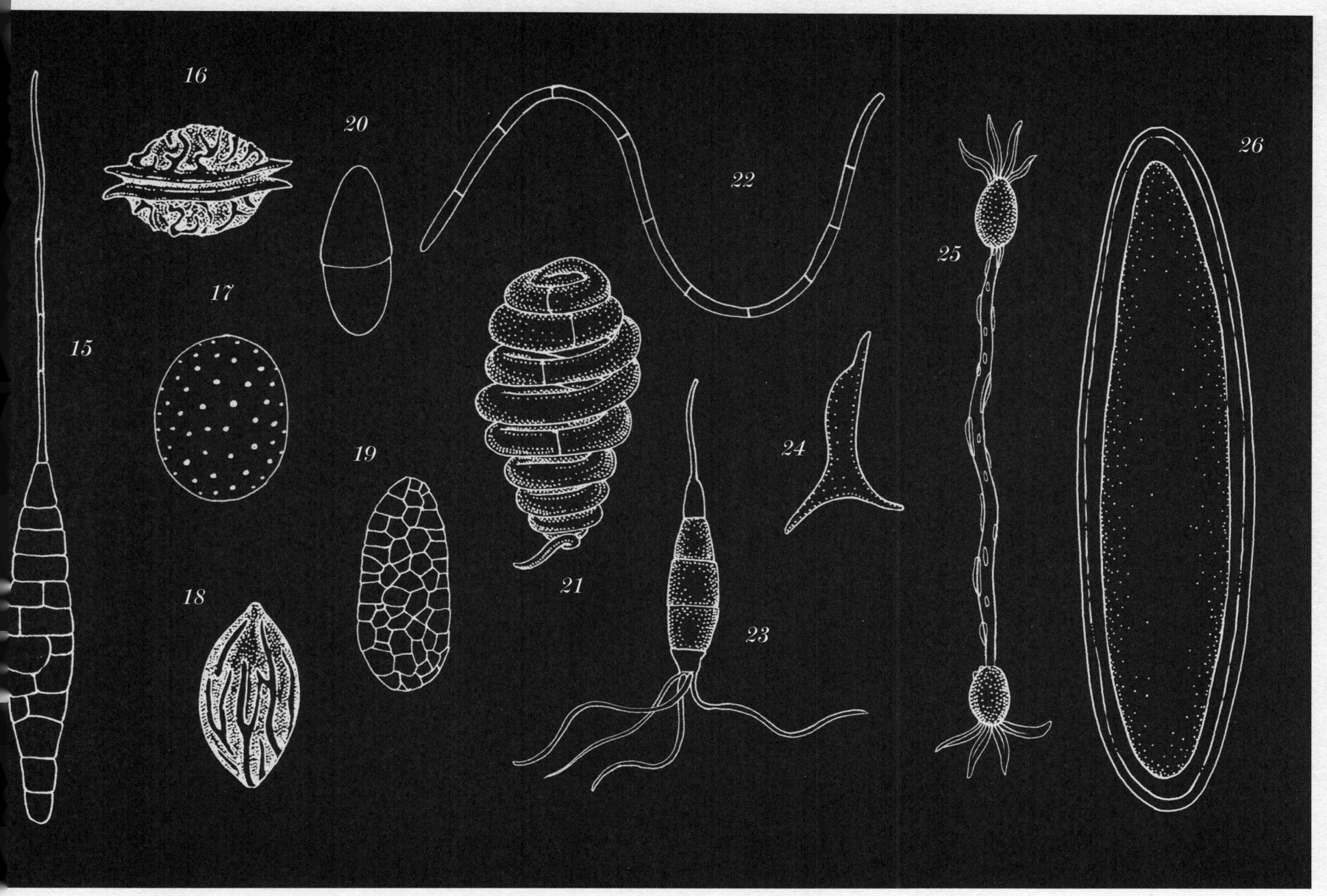

travel 20 inches/50 centimeters or more, while others split into part-spores to increase the number of dispersal units (propagules) and establish new colonies. There is a misunderstanding that fungal spores are easily distributed in the air. In reality most do not travel far at all on their own, as they are formed too close to the ground. Some are specially adapted to dispersal by insects, birds, or mammals. Truffles, for example, produce their spores in sporing bodies below ground that release a special aroma that attracts mammals, which help dispersal. Some elaborate spores with long arms are adapted to disperse in water.

Key to plate

1: Helicomyces scandens (20 μm)
2: Podospora fimiseda (360 μm)
3: Xerocomus badius (12 μm)
4: Sporormiella leporina (35 μm)
5: Schizoxylon ligustri (125 μm)
6: Russula viridofusca (12 μm)
7: Harknessia spermatoidea (120 μm)
8: Ustilago koenigiae (12 μm)
9: Tetrachaetum elegans (250 μm)
10: Caryospora callicarpa (75 μm)
11: Lophotrichus ampullus (10 μm)
12: Triangularia bambusae (25 μm)
13: Rinodina confragosula (28 μm)
14: Corollospora lacera (65 μm)
15: Alternaria sesami (400 μm)
16: Penicillium baarnense (6 μm)
17: Gelasinospora micropertusa (40 μm)
18: Neurospora lineolata (20 μm)
19: Calenia monospora (65 μm)
20: Neonectria ditissima (12 μm)
21: Helicoon ellipticum (40 μm)
22: Anguillospora longissima (240 μm)
23: Pestalotiopsis guepinii (45 μm)
24: Cornutispora lichenicola (15 μm)
25: Zygopleurage zygospora (285 μm)
26: Pertusaria pertusa (220 μm)

Note: measurements shown are length or longest axis

FUNGAL BIOLOGY

Growth

All filamentous fungi are made from narrow, cylindrical tubes called hyphae. These are usually less than ten micrometers wide and have tough walls containing chitin (page 8). Hyphae are filled with liquid kept under high pressure by taking in water through their walls. Most are divided by inner walls so that they look like the cells of animals and plants, but their internal structures, called organelles, can move freely through compartments as the cell contents flow through the hyphae. They grow from their tips, which contain specific organelles that generate new wall tissue. Masses of branching hyphae together form what is known as a mycelium.

Hyphae can act like hydraulic rams, puncturing the surfaces of leaves, forcing themselves through soils and wood, and even penetrating rock surfaces—aided by the release of enzymes or organic acids from their tips that break down material as they grow. Their branching patterns vary according to the availability of food, becoming dense in a radial manner when they find nutrients. Sometimes they twist themselves into whitish ropelike cords or dark-brown bootlace-like strands called rhizomorphs.

Not all fungi form hyphae all of the time, or in some cases at all. Yeasts are single-celled and divide repeatedly by "budding," forming mounded, circular superficial colonies. Some can also produce hyphae when invading tissues, while filamentous fungi can have yeast-like stages in their life cycles. Chytrids living in moist or aquatic environments are almost invariably single-celled and never form colonies.

Growth rates vary enormously. Humidity and temperature are the key—species have optimal conditions to match their ecology. Pin molds such as *Mucor* species can cover a slice of damp bread in a few days, while a lichen fungus on a rock may increase only a few millimeters a year. Human pathogens grow best at body temperature, while fungi of hot deserts favor temperatures around 100°F/45°C.

Growth rates are of practical importance too. They can help date how long an object (even a corpse) has been in a place or, in the case of lichens, when a roof was built or a glacial moraine was deposited—a technique known as lichenometry by glaciologists.

Key to plate

1: **Blue mold rot fungus on apple**
Penicillium expansum
When growing on a nutrient-rich surface like an apple, the hyphae of this fungi branch repeatedly in a radial manner, forming circular patches. In some fungi, if there is a shortage of nutrients, the hyphae will spread out and forage for something to digest, and when they find it will concentrate around it.

2: **Toxic black mold**
Stachybotrys chartarum
Pictured growing on cellulosic material

Characterized by conidia that can be seen under a lens, this species occurs in warm, damp conditions and can be found in homes and buildings. It is one of a complex of species that has been linked to health issues in humans and animals.

3: ***Trichoderma viride***
Pictured on a culture plate, displaying typical radial growth

Some fast-growing species of this genus can be cultivated to combat the spread of fungal pathogens in various plants, including cotton, tobacco, and sugarcane.

FUNGAL BIOLOGY

Ecosystem: Mountains

From peak to base and across snow-covered landscapes, bare stone, and luscious forests, mountains provide a diverse range of environments in which many different fungi occur; some of them cannot be found anywhere else in the world. The fungi that live here need to adapt to the severe conditions that become harsher with increasing elevation. Above the tree line, the alpine zone is characterized by short, open vegetation (mostly grasses and small woody plants), low temperatures, and high exposure to sun and wind. Here, the ground is covered by snow most of the year. At lower elevations, conditions are less harsh, and trees can grow in deeper and richer soils. The environmental characteristics in each zone shape the communities of fungi and plants that exist there.

At high altitudes, ectomycorrhizal fungi—ones that form symbiotic (mutually beneficial) relationships with the roots of plants—are essential for the survival of small alpine woody plants like species of dwarf willows (*Salix*) and mountain avens (*Dryas octopetala*), as well as herbaceous plants like the alpine bistort (*Bistorta vivipara*) and false sedge (*Kobresia simpliciuscula*). The most abundant ectomycorrhizal fungi in alpine habitats above the tree line include webcaps (*Cortinarius*), fibercaps (*Inocybe*), poison pies (*Hebeloma*), deceivers (*Laccaria*), pinkgills (*Entoloma*), milkcaps (*Lactarius*), and brittlegills (*Russula*), all of which form gilled mushrooms. Less familiar and detectable, but equally abundant, are crust-like fungi including *Tomentella* and some *Sebacina* species, found under rocks or on soil or decaying wood. Above the tree line, lichens can dominate, growing on exposed rock surfaces.

Below the tree line and in the litter layer of forests (made up of mainly dead plant material on the surface of the soil), other mycorrhizal fungi (those that form relationships with plants generally) such as boletes like *Suillus* and *Leccinum* can be seen, alongside decomposers such as jelly fungi (*Calocera,* stagshorns). The stinking parachute (*Gymnopus perforans*), a tiny marasmioid (Marasmius-looking) fungus, can also be found in forests.

Key to plate

1: **Alpine webcap**
Cortinarius alpinus
Shown here forming a symbiotic relationship with the roots of the dwarf willow *Salix herbacea*, the alpine webcap grows taller than its plant host.

2: **Alpine brittlegill**
Russula nana
This beautiful small mushroom forms a symbiotic relationship with the roots of the alpine bistort, *Bistorta vivipara*. It can also live in symbiosis with other Arctic or alpine plant species.

3: **Favre s fibercap**
Inocybe favrei
This mushroom forms a symbiotic relationship with the roots of mountain avens (*Dryas octopetala*), seen here. It is named after the pioneering Swiss geologist Jules Favre.

4: **Gassy webcap**
Cortinarius traganus
This violet mushroom is well known for its strong, unpleasant scent. It forms symbiotic relationships with roots of pine and birch trees.

5: **Yellow stagshorn**
Calocera viscosa
This fiery-bright fungus grows in dead wood. *Calocera* means "beautiful and waxy," while *viscosa* means "sticky"— fitting as this fungus can be used as a chewing gum.

6: **Stinking parachute**
Gymnopus perforans
These miniature fungi form sporing bodies around fallen conifer needles. Despite their small size, they smell strongly of rotten cabbage.

7: **Weeping bolete**
Suillus granulatus
With a greasy cap and dots on the stem, this mushroom forms a symbiotic relationship with the roots of pine trees. When young, it releases milky droplets, which give it its name.

8: **Orange birch bolete**
Leccinum versipelle
This large bolete forms a symbiotic relationship only with birch trees.

FUNGARIUM

Gallery 2

Fungal Diversity

Cup Fungi
Mushrooms and Toadstools
Bracket Fungi
Gasteromycetes
Foliicolous Fungi
Ecosystem: Temperate Forests

FUNGAL DIVERSITY

Cup Fungi

Cup-shaped sporing bodies, often known as apothecia, are produced by a wide range of groups within the fungal kingdom, mostly belonging to the ascomycetes. Despite their relatively simple structure, they have an enormous variety of forms, many of which are eye-catching and beautiful. Some are extremely tiny (less than a millimeter in diameter) and can be seen clearly only with a hand lens or microscope, while others can reach 4 inches/10 centimeters or more. They are often brightly colored, and some have short or long stalks, while others have eyelash-like hairs. Many lichens also produce tiny cups to spread their spores.

Most cup fungi are spore shooters. The inside of the cup is lined with spore-bearing tissue, and when the cup is mature and the weather conditions are just right, spores are shot out at high speed in a synchronized puff. In some of the larger cup fungi, dispersal can be triggered by blowing on them, resulting in the release of a smoky cloud of spores.

Because the sporing bodies of most cup fungi are fleshy and soft, they are prone to drying out. These species prefer damp habitats and are intolerant of dry conditions, although there are exceptions. This diverse group is found in a wide range of habitats, from beaches to scorched earth, from animal dung to dead plant matter, and can even appear on carpets and the walls of houses. Most live and feed on dead plant material or soil and in turn become food for other organisms such as insects. Some even form mutually beneficial relationships with tree roots or with plants such as mosses. One group has evolved to catch tiny eelworms with sticky knobs or lassos.

Key to plate

1: **Spring orange peel fungus**
Caloscypha fulgens
This golden-colored species is named for its appearance, which resembles discarded fruit peel.

2: ***Plectania chilensis***
This fungus occurs on wood in the Southern Hemisphere.

3: **Scarlet elf cap**
Sarcoscypha austriaca
The name of this vibrant species means "from Austria," where it is commonly found, although it also occurs in other parts of Europe and North America. It thrives on decaying organic matter and in damp conditions among mosses and leaf litter.

4: ***Cookeina speciosa***
This beautiful pinkish-red fungus forms sporing bodies that look like velvety goblets. It is found in the forests of the neotropics growing on rotting wood on the forest floor.

5: **Eyelash fungus**
Scutellinia scutellata
This fungus's bright disks have black eyelash-like hairs along the margin that fold inward over much of the disk when conditions are dry. It is often found on damp, rotten timber on woodland floors. Several similar species differ in the details of their spores.

6: **Orange peel fungus**
Aleuria aurantia
This fungus begins as a cup shape, but twists and contorts itself, often splitting in the process, making it resemble an orange peel.

7: **Hare's ear**
Otidea onotica
Found in many parts of Europe and North America, this golden-colored fungus commonly lines the pathways of well-trodden routes through temperate woodland.

8: **Black earth tongue**
Trichoglossum hirsutum
Velvety in texture and with spear-headed sporing bodies, this darkly colored fungus occurs in acidic soils.

9: **Green elf cup**
Chlorociboria aeruginosa
This species produces a vivid blue-green pigment that stains the wood it's growing on. Historically, this wood was used in decorative woodwork known as Tunbridge ware.

FUNGAL DIVERSITY

Mushrooms and Toadstools

When people think about fungi, they usually envisage mushrooms or toadstools. These are the fleshy sporing bodies often seen growing in soil or on wood. Mushrooms and toadstools come in all colors of the rainbow and in many different sizes: from the tiny purple *Cortinarius bibulus*, with a cap diameter of about 5 millimeters, to *Termitomyces titanicus*, which is 200 times larger and whose cap can measure up to 3 feet/1 meter across.

Mushroom and *toadstool* are not scientific terms but are used to describe sporing bodies with a similar appearance. They can belong to many orders of fungi. The sporing bodies we call mushrooms are fleshy and have a cap, gills, and a stem. Sometimes the word *mushroom* is used for edible fungi, while the word *toadstool* is usually applied to fungi that are inedible or poisonous. The best known of these is the striking red-and-white fly agaric (*Amanita muscaria*). The term *toadstool* originates from the medieval idea that toads, considered carriers of poison, liked to sit on these sporing bodies.

An interesting phenomenon unique to mushrooms and toadstools is the formation of "fairy rings." which occur when mushrooms or toadstools grow in an arc or circle. Fairy rings can be found in woodlands and grasslands and are produced by more than fifty different species, including the edible fairy ring fungus (*Marasmius oreades*). The center of the ring is where the fungus has started its growth. The ring of sporing bodies is produced outside the edge of the fungus's growing structure, called the mycelium.

One of the most colorful mushroom groups is the waxcaps (*Hygrocybe* spp.). The sporing bodies of waxcaps come in wonderful shades of red, orange, and yellow, while some species are green or pinkish purple. Some of them are found only on nutrient-poor grasslands, habitats that are declining. In the United Kingdom, the growth of waxcaps on grassland is used as a measure of whether the site should be legally protected.

Key to plate

1: **Shaggy ink cap**
Coprinus comatus
This species is often found on lawns. It grows in groups and has a beautiful scaly white cap, with gills that secrete a black "ink" when maturing. This fungus can kill and digest roundworms for extra nutrition.

2: **Fly agaric**
Amanita muscaria
This widespread species has been used to catch flies and also in religious rituals by shamans because of its hallucinogenic properties.

3: **Shaggy scalycap**
Pholiota squarrosa
This common parasitic fungus can be found growing in clusters at the base of stumps and trees. It is covered in scales, which makes it easy to recognize.

4: **Violet webcap**
Cortinarius violaceus
The easiest *Cortinarius* species to recognize, this beautiful big violet mushroom occurs in Europe and North America.

5: **Blue roundhead**
Stropharia caerulea
Because of its blue coloring, this species is easy to spot. It is a saprophyte, meaning it doesn't need a host tree and instead gains nutrition from decaying organic matter.

6: **Waxcaps**
Hygrocybe spp.
(a, b, c, d) As shown here, waxcaps are bright spots of color; they are often seen on long-established grasslands and lawns. Some grassland waxcaps are especially rare.

FUNGAL DIVERSITY

Bracket Fungi

While most mushrooms produce their spores inside gills, bracket fungi (or polypores) form sporing bodies with pores or tubes on their underside. In most cases, they are as hard as the wood of the trees they grow on. They make shelf-shaped, bracket-shaped, or—more rarely—circular bodies that are often called conks. Like most mushrooms, they belong to the phylum Basidiomycota, and it seems that they have appeared independently multiple times in the evolution of the fungal kingdom.

Bracket fungi are wood decayers, growing mainly on tree trunks and branches, but a few exceptions can form mycorrhizas, or symbiotic relationships, with tree roots. They are the only organisms able to break down the tough compounds that make up lignin, a substance found in wood, so without bracket fungi (and their relatives, corticioid fungi, or crust fungi, which grow mostly on the undersides of dead tree trunks or branches), forests would be covered in wood and leaf litter! That is why they are vital for nutrient cycling and carbon dioxide release in forest ecosystems. On the other hand, some of them are severe pathogens of trees and major causes of damage to timber.

But bracket fungi are not only important for ecosystems; they have also been used by humans since ancient times. The tinder fungus (*Fomes fomentarius*), a common and widely distributed species, is easy to find and recognize and has been used to make clothing such as caps. It is best known, however, for its application as tinder. The species was found with Ötzi the Iceman, a mummified prehistoric person found in Europe's Ötztal Alps. It is thought that he may have been carrying it to make fire.

Another bracket fungus used by humans is chaga (*Inonotus obliquus*). It is believed to suppress cancer progression and enhance our immune system. This species looks like burnt coal and can be found growing on the trunks of mature birch trees.

Some bracket fungi can be used to indicate that a forest is ancient. These species are very sensitive to the impact of human activities; once they have disappeared, they may never return, and some may become extinct.

Key to plate

1: **Giant elm bracket**
Rigidoporus ulmarius
This fungal pathogen grows mostly on broad-leaved trees such as elm. The brackets are usually whitish to cream, but they often become green due to the growth of green algae. For many years, a bracket of *Rigidoporus ulmarius* in Kew Gardens was the largest known fungus ever discovered, with a circumference of about 16 feet/5 meters. Bracket fungi generally grow concentrically and often show bands of growth.

2: **Beefsteak fungus**
Fistulina hepatica
As its common name indicates, this species has the appearance of raw meat. It was actually used as a meat substitute in the past; it has a fleshy consistency and bleeds a red juice when cut. Its underside is a white mass of tiny tubes (a reduction of the typical gills). Its Latin species name, *hepatica*, means "liver-like."

3: **Oak polypore**
Buglossoporus quercinus
Underside of bracket
This rare polypore is found on ancient oaks in old-growth woodlands and pastures where exposed heartwood is present. Given their slow growth, narrow range of environmental conditions, and shrinking habitats, this species is under threat and has the highest level of legal protection in the United Kingdom. It has recently been added to the IUCN Red List of Threatened Species.

1 
2 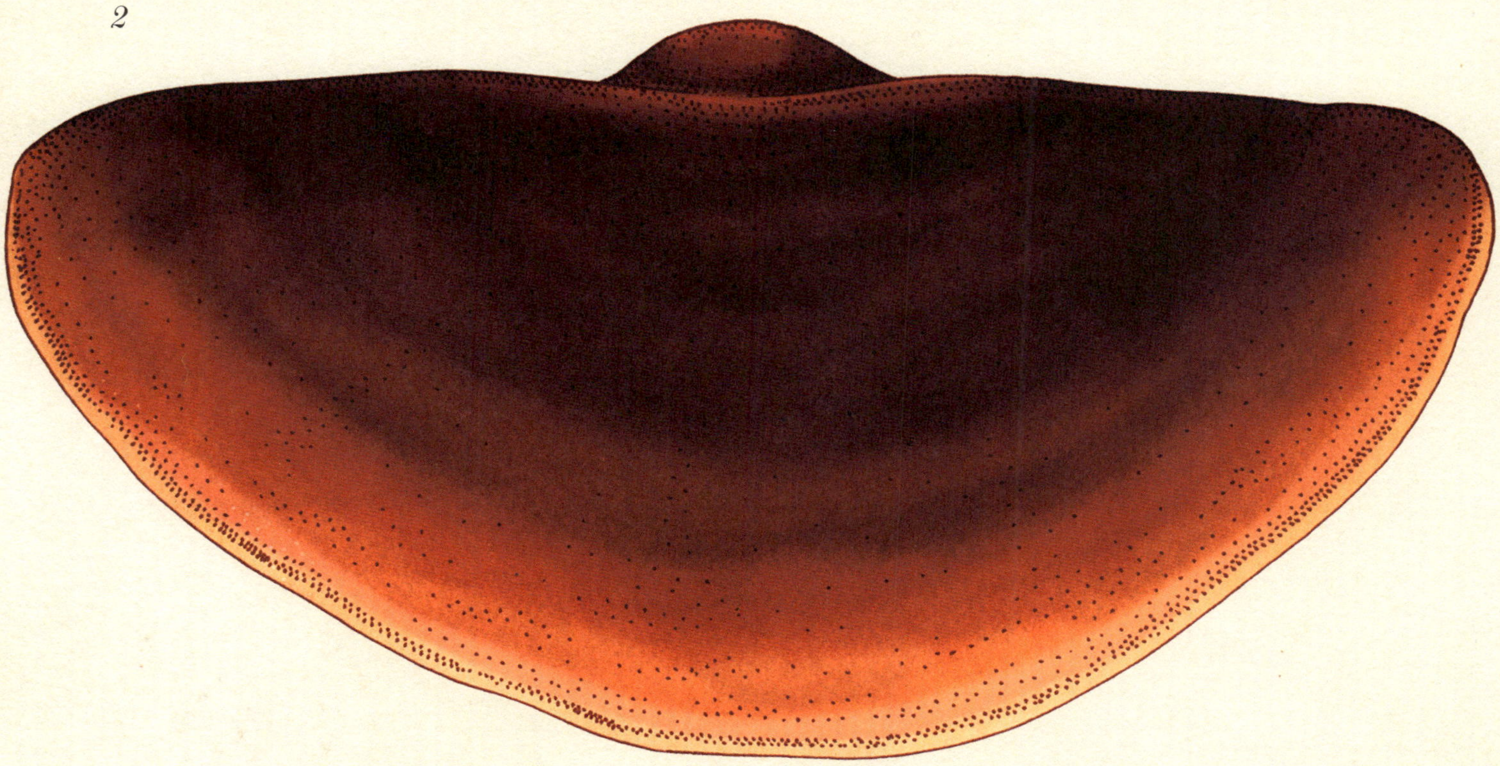
3

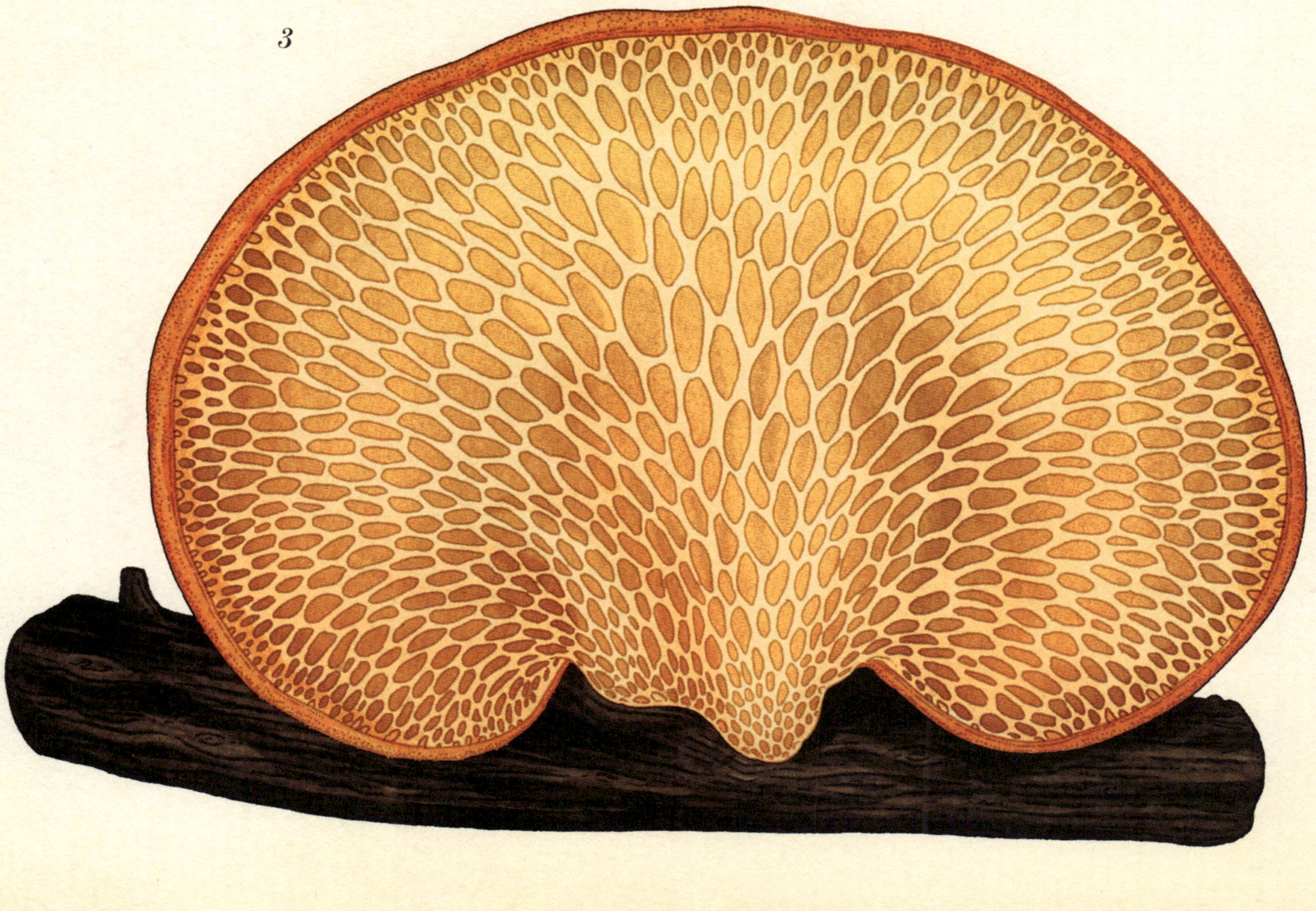

FUNGAL DIVERSITY

Gasteromycetes

Gasteromycetes are fungi that share similar reproductive strategies, even though they are not closely related. Often, though not always, they are saprophytic, meaning they derive their food by breaking down organic material in the soil. In doing so they play an important role in the ecosystem because they recycle nutrients.

Unlike other mushroom-forming fungi, gasteromycetes do not have the ability to forcibly disperse their spores from gills or pores. They produce spores on the inside of their sporing bodies and have developed different strategies to disperse them. This has led to the evolution of unusual and strikingly beautiful mushroom forms.

The simplest kinds of spore dispersal take place in puffballs. These fungi have round sporing bodies ranging in size from just a few millimeters wide to something bigger than a watermelon. In some, the spore-rich mass on their inside needs physical contact to be ejected. This can be anything from falling raindrops to more vigorous actions such as being knocked by an animal walking past. Some puffballs have small holes out of which spore masses can be puffed out; others simply split open. Earthstars have evolved a similar appearance to puffballs, with a small pore at the top, out of which spores are released when touched.

Bird's-nest fungi make use of raindrops to disperse their spores. Their sporing bodies are shaped like specialized "splash cups," and the spores held in sacs at the base look like eggs. Raindrops hitting the inside of the cup force the spore sacs to be ejected. In some cases, the sacs are eaten by animals and so are further dispersed—and fertilized—in their dung.

Complex and unusual spore-forming bodies are found in the stinkhorn fungi. This weird and wonderful family produces a brownish, spore-rich liquid called gleba over their surfaces. Gleba is foul-smelling—like rotting meat and feces—and attracts insects who like these food sources. The insects disperse the spores when they fly away with gleba stuck to them.

Key to plate

1: **Common puffball**
Lycoperdon perlatum
The cream-colored outer flesh of this fungus is covered with tiny bumps and spikes and becomes brown when mature. At this stage, a small pore opens at the apex, which the spores burst from.

2: **Sculpted puffball**
Calvatia sculpta
This unusual-looking puffball has pyramid-shaped growths on its outer surface, through which spores are released.

3: **Bird's-nest fungus**
Cyathus striatus
This widespread fungus can often be found growing on mulch and compost in gardens and holds its spores in pellet-like sacs called peridioles.

4: **Stinkhorn fungus**
Colus hirudinosus
The cage-like structure of this fungus intensifies from a light orange at the base to a dark red at the tip and emerges from a gelatinous white "egg." Despite its beauty, it has an odor similar to feces. It is edible.

5: **Earthstar fungus**
Geastrum quadrifidum
The earthstar's sporing body starts out as a small gray-brown ball, then the outer layer splits into a star-shaped base, which exposes the central spore case and thrusts it upward, where it can more easily disperse the spores.

6: **Rounded earthstar**
Geastrum saccatum
The immature egg-shaped sporing body of this species eventually splits, with the outer layer curving to the base to reveal a spore case at the center. It is found throughout the world.

7: **Veiled lady**
Phallus indusiatus
The delicate veil around the sporing body of this striking-looking fungus, a member of the stinkhorn family, doesn't disguise the fact that it smells truly foul.

8: **Common earthball**
Scleroderma citrinum
(a) Unlike most other gasteromycetes, this fungus is mycorrhizal, forming symbiotic relationships with the roots of some trees and shrubs.
(b) When opened, it reveals dark, purple-black gleba and is toxic if eaten.

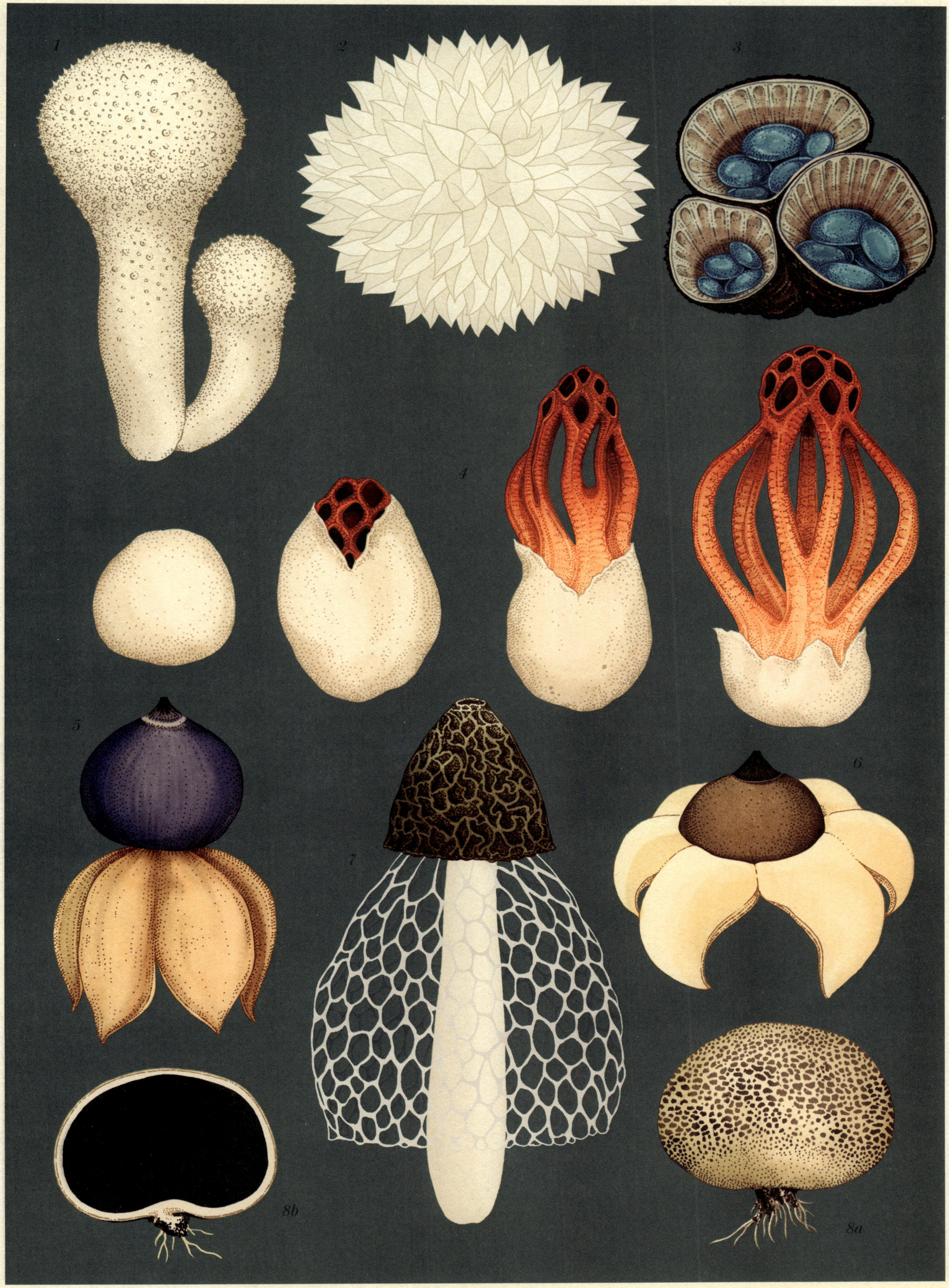
1
2
3
4
5
6
7
8b
8a

Foliicolous Fungi

In tropical forests, many leaves look like they have beautiful mosaics on their surfaces. These are mostly fungi. In these habitats, trees are evergreen and individual leaves can be very large and live for many years. A wide variety of fungi have evolved that use them as places to live. Unlike plant pathogenic fungi, they do so harmlessly.

These benign fungi are known as foliicolous. They do not penetrate the living cells of the leaves they grow on. Some types have special bodies by which they attach themselves to a leaf's surface; others grow between the plant cuticle (a protective film covering the leaf) and the living parts of the leaf's surface layer. Foliicolous fungi gain nutrients not from the leaves they grow on but from water that drips from the forest canopy. A number are lichen-forming and capture leaf-dwelling green algae to secure a supply of sugars. Since non-lichen fungi do not photosynthesize and therefore don't need light, some groups grow only on the underside of leaves.

Many foliicolous fungi form rosettes, made up of shield-like, radiating hyphae covering their spore-producing structures. These superficial hyphae are often dark brown to black, which helps them resist becoming dried out in times of drought. When viewed with a lens, these are often visible as delicate networks crisscrossing the leaf surface.

There are concerns that excessive growths of these organisms can adversely affect tree health, such as in oil palm and tea plantations, but some studies in Australia suggest that colonized leaves compensate by producing more chlorophyll in their uncolonized parts. Foliicolous fungi are also an important habitat for other fungi that live only on particular foliicolous species, and seem to be benign. While foliiculous fungi are mainly a feature of the humid tropics, a few species are able to grow in temperate regions on evergreen leaves, including box, holly, juniper, and laurel.

Key to plate

1: **Meliola urariae**
Some of this fungus's branches are composed of hyphopodia, one-lobed cells that attach the fungus to a leaf and help absorb food. Species in the family Meliolaceae mostly live symbiotically on leaves and stems of particular plants.

2: **Leaf**
Seen with a mixture of fungal colonies on its surface, including some lichens.

3: **Strigula orbicularis**
(a) Sporing bodies and thallus, or main fungus body
(b) Section of a sporing body with plant cuticle layer on top and epidermal cells in a layer below

4: **Tricharia urceolata**
This lichen is strictly tropical and is abundant in South America. Species of *Tricharia* produce hair-like structures called hyphophores, which produce asexual spores called conidia.

5: **Parenglerula macowanianus**
(a) Example of mycelium growth on a leaf with hyphopodia and dark rounded sporing bodies
(b) Section of a sporing body growing on a leaf surface showing several spore sacs, one of which is full of spores

6: **Shield fungus**
Lichenopeltella palustris
This fungus's specialized flattened sporing body has a wall of quadrangular cells arranged in radiating rows that grow on the leaf and a central rounded aperture called an ostiole, which is crowned by black hair-like structures through which spores are released.

7: **Peltistroma juruanum**
Colonies of this fungus are shown here growing on a section of a leaf.

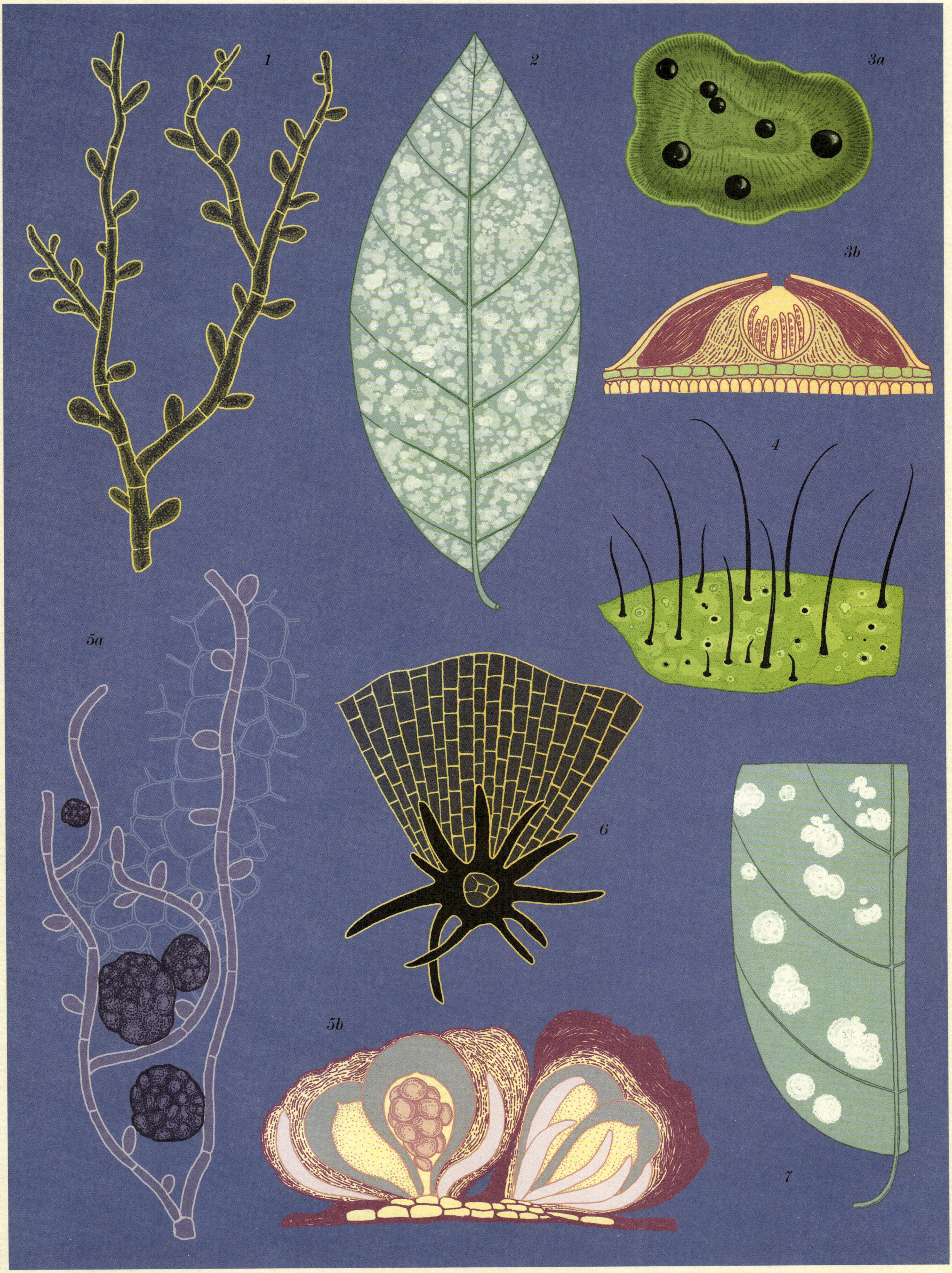
1
2
3a
3b
4
5a
6
5b
7

FUNGAL DIVERSITY

Ecosystem: Temperate Forests

With fertile soils, plenty of rain, and seasonal weather, temperate forests make ideal homes for fungi. Oak and beech are common deciduous trees in these forests, and they harbor a significant portion of fungi. Forest fungi play important roles: saprotrophs break down organic matter, ectomycorrhizal fungi enhance tree growth by forming symbiotic relationships with roots, and various fungi associate with algae or cyanobacteria to form lichens.

Some saprotrophs grow in the roots of trees. These include the zoned rosette (*Podoscypha multizonata*), which forms coral-like concentric fans, and the gilled mushroom spindle toughshank (*Gymnopus fusipes*). Others can be found on trunk heartwood (the dense, inner core of the trunk), on lower branches of living trees, and on fallen wood. Examples of these include chicken of the woods (*Laetiporus sulphureus*), a bracket fungus that causes brown rot and occurs on trunks, and beefsteak fungus (*Fistulina hepatica*), with its liver-like red brackets. *Mycena inclinata* is a saprotroph that is usually found on fallen branches; it is recognizable by its distinctive oily and soapy smell.

In temperate ecosystems, fungi can also signal environmental conditions. The oak milkcap (*Lactarius quietus*) is an indicator of high nitrogen pollution and soil acidification, two of the main threats to temperate forests, while the tree lungwort lichen (*Lobaria pulmonaria*) thrives in ancient woodlands with low pollution levels, making it a good indicator of clean habitats.

Key to plate

1: **Oakmoss lichen**
Evernia prunastri
Found growing on the trunk and twigs of trees and shrubs, this decoratively branched lichen resembles deer antlers.

2: **Chicken of the woods**
Laetiporus sulphureus
So-called because its texture and consistency are similar to cooked chicken.

3: **Beefsteak fungus**
Fistulina hepatica
(previously described on page 26)

4: **Zoned rosette**
Podoscypha multizonata
This striking, rare fungus grows on soil around oak trees.

5: **Spindle toughshank**
Gymnopus fusipes
This common species is usually found in clumps where the tree trunk meets the soil and causes root rot in oaks. It grows among roots from dormant, hardened structures called sclerotia.

6: **Oak milkcap**
Lactarius quietus
The oak milkcap lives in symbiosis with the roots of oak trees. When cut or torn, its gills release a milky latex.

7: **Clustered bonnet**
Mycena inclinata
This mushroom is a saprotroph often found on fallen branches.

8: **Yellowfoot or trumpet chanterelle**
Craterellus tubaeformis
Appearing in large groups, these edible chanterelles form ectomycorrhizas with the roots of oaks. This makes it very difficult to grow them commercially.

9: **Coral fungi**
Ramaria sp.
This fungus occurs abundantly in temperate forests, forming coral-like sporing bodies on soil.

10: **Beech or slimy milkcap**
Lactarius blennius
This fungus lives in association with the roots of beech trees and is native to Europe. *Blennius* means "slimy" and describes the cap's surface.

11: **Common earthball**
Scleroderma citrinum
This ectomycorrhizal fungus forms relationships with oak and beech roots in acidic soils. The inner part of the body contains dark spores.

12: **Matte bolete**
Xerocomellus pruinatus
This bolete is native to Europe and lives in association with the roots of beech and oak trees. It produces mushrooms that, under the cap, have yellow tubes that end in pores instead of gills, which harbor the spores.

13: **Tree lungwort lichen**
Lobaria pulmonaria
This lung-shaped lichen is formed by three different organisms: a fungus, an alga, and a cyanobacterium.

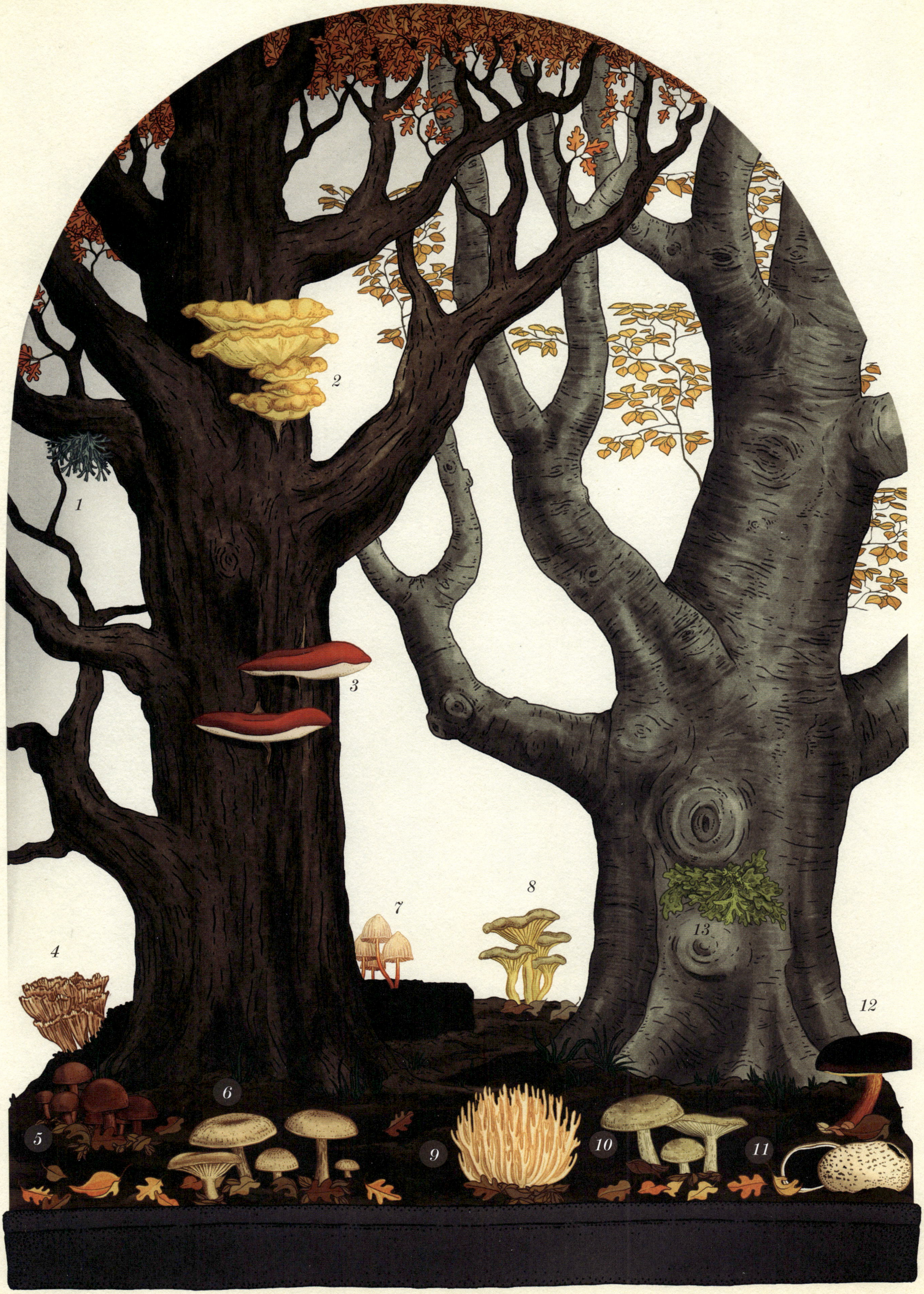
1
2
3
4
5
6
7
8
9
10
11
12
13

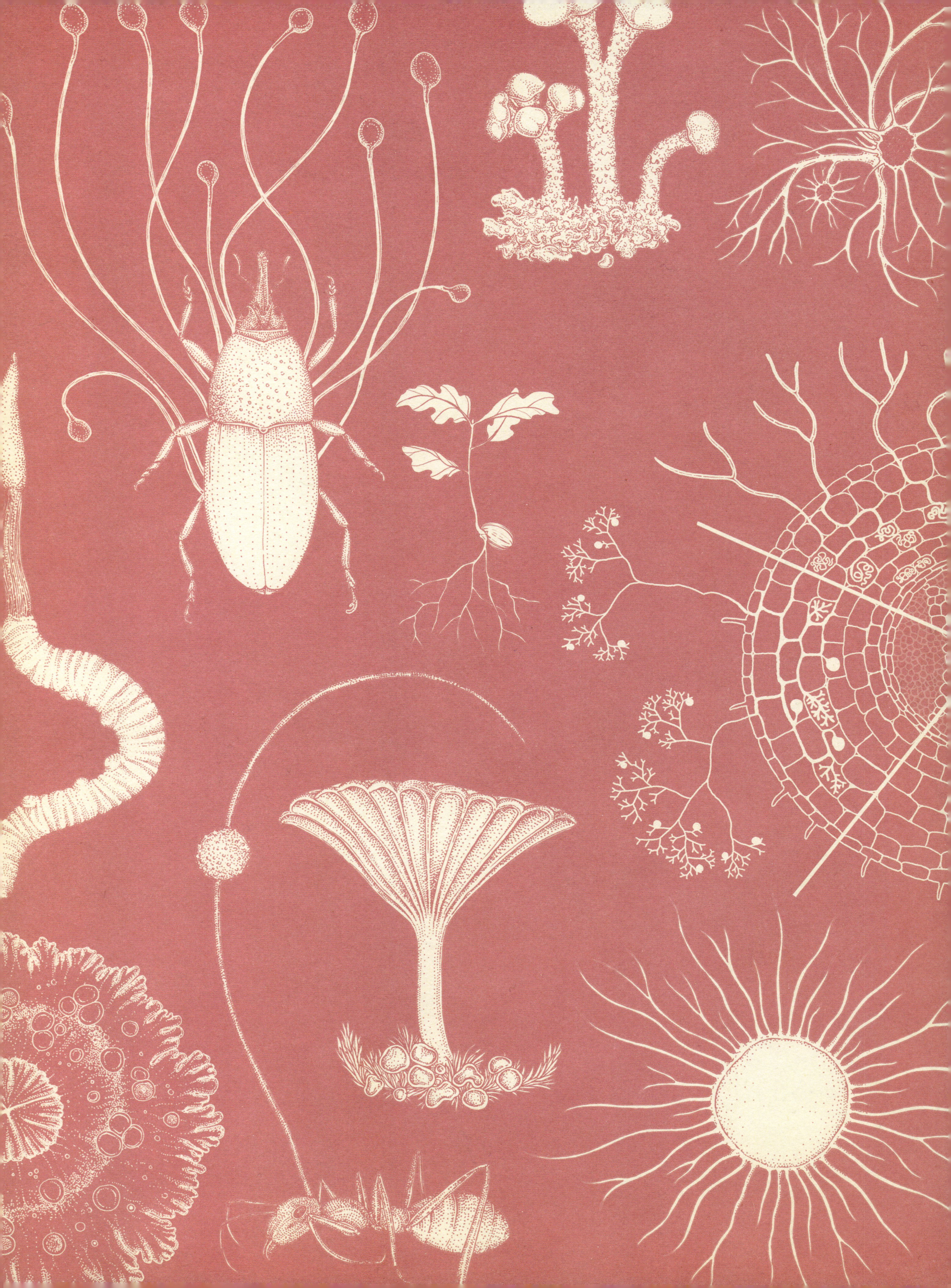

FUNGARIUM

Gallery 3

Fungal Interactions

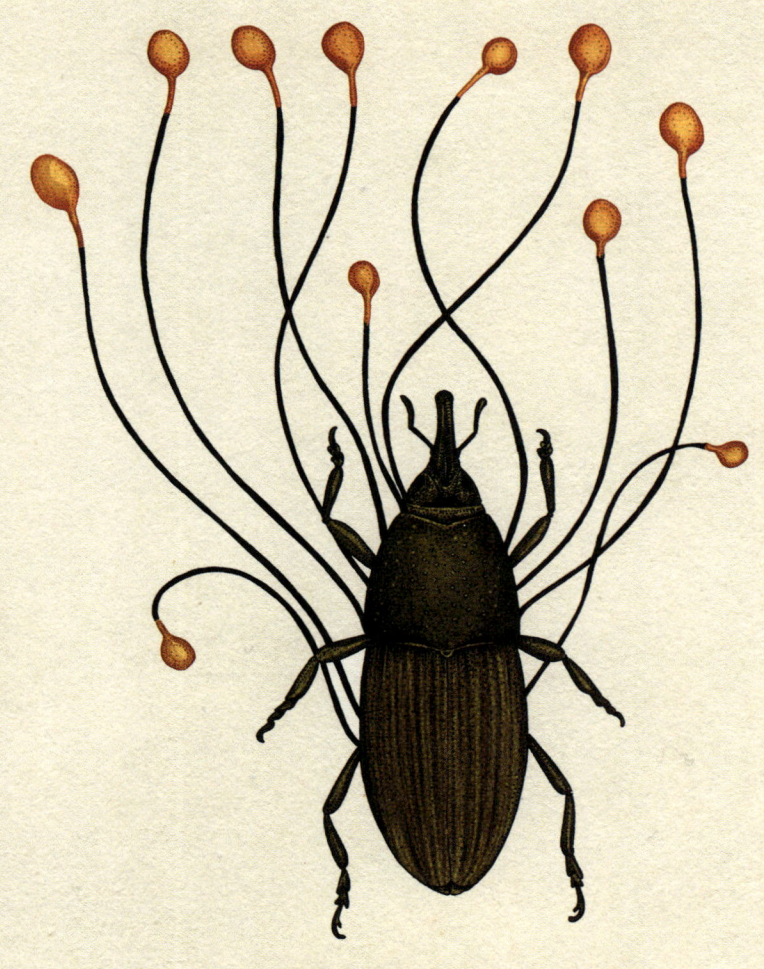

Mycorrhizas
Mycorrhizal Networks
Lichens
Entomogenous Fungi
Ants and Termites

FUNGAL INTERACTIONS

Mycorrhizas

Hidden to our eyes most of the time and living in the soil under our feet, there are fungi that form associations called mycorrhizas with plant roots. These associations are symbiotic, or mutually beneficial, and occur between certain fungi and most plants on Earth. These relationships evolved millions of years ago and helped the first plants establish themselves on land and successfully grow in nutrient-poor environments. Even now, 90 percent of the plants on Earth cannot live without these fungi in their roots!

Mycorrhizal fungi colonize the roots of plants. They provide the plants with water and nutrients from the soil that the plants cannot obtain themselves. In return, the fungi obtain plant carbohydrates that they need to grow. Different fungi associate with different plants, forming four main types of mycorrhizas: arbuscular mycorrhizas, ectomycorrhizas, ericoid mycorrhizas, and orchid mycorrhizas.

Around 80 percent of all plants (including fruit trees, most grasses, and food crops) form arbuscular mycorrhizas, which specialize in absorbing phosphorus from soil. This nutrient is limited in the soils where these plants grow. Only around 2 percent of plants form associations with ectomycorrhizal fungi, including many edible ones like chanterelles, truffles, and porcini. These fungi specialize in the uptake of nitrogen and associate with woody plants, including oaks, pines, beech, and gum trees. Ericoid mycorrhizal fungi colonize the roots of plants of the Ericaceae family (including heathers, blueberries, and rhododendrons) and some liverworts, unlocking nutrients for their host plants. Orchids are also dependent on mycorrhizal fungi and cannot germinate without them. They need these fungi in their first stages of development as well.

Key to plate

1: **Cross section of a root showing the four main types of mycorrhizas**
(a) Arbuscular mycorrhizas
The fungal filaments form structures called arbuscules and/or vesicles (sacs for storage) inside the plant root cells.
(b) Ectomycorrhizas
The fungal filaments surround the feeder roots, forming a sheath of fungal tissue called the mantle and extending into the soil. They also grow between the roots' cells, forming what's called the "Hartig net," where the nutrient exchange between fungus and plant takes place.
(c) Ericoid mycorrhizas
The fungal filaments penetrate the root cell walls, forming coils. This mycorrhizal type is abundant in heathlands, tundra, and boreal ecosystems, where the fungi help the plants to compete for nutrients in very poor soils.
(d) Orchid mycorrhizas
The fungal filaments penetrate the root cell walls and form coils called pelotons that can be reabsorbed by the plant. The seeds of orchids do not have nutrients, so orchids rely on these fungi to germinate.
(e) Nonmycorrhizal
Root with no fungal tissue present

2: **Cenococcum geophilum**
(a) This ascomycete has one name but actually comprises a complex of species that colonize the roots of over 200 different plant hosts, forming ectomycorrhizas. They are easily spotted because of their black color and thick fungal filaments.
(b) Despite being abundant in the roots, these fungi do not form sporing bodies, but they can remain in soil for hundreds of years in the form of dormant structures called sclerotia, as shown here.

3. **Saffron milkcap**
Lactarius deliciosus
(a) This is how this fungus looks in the roots of pine, forming ectomycorrhizas. Its ectomycorrhizas are characterized by their smooth bright-orange surfaces and the dichotomous branching pattern of the pine.
(b) The orange mushroom is the edible sporing body and is seen only in autumn. Its gills release orange latex when torn or cut.

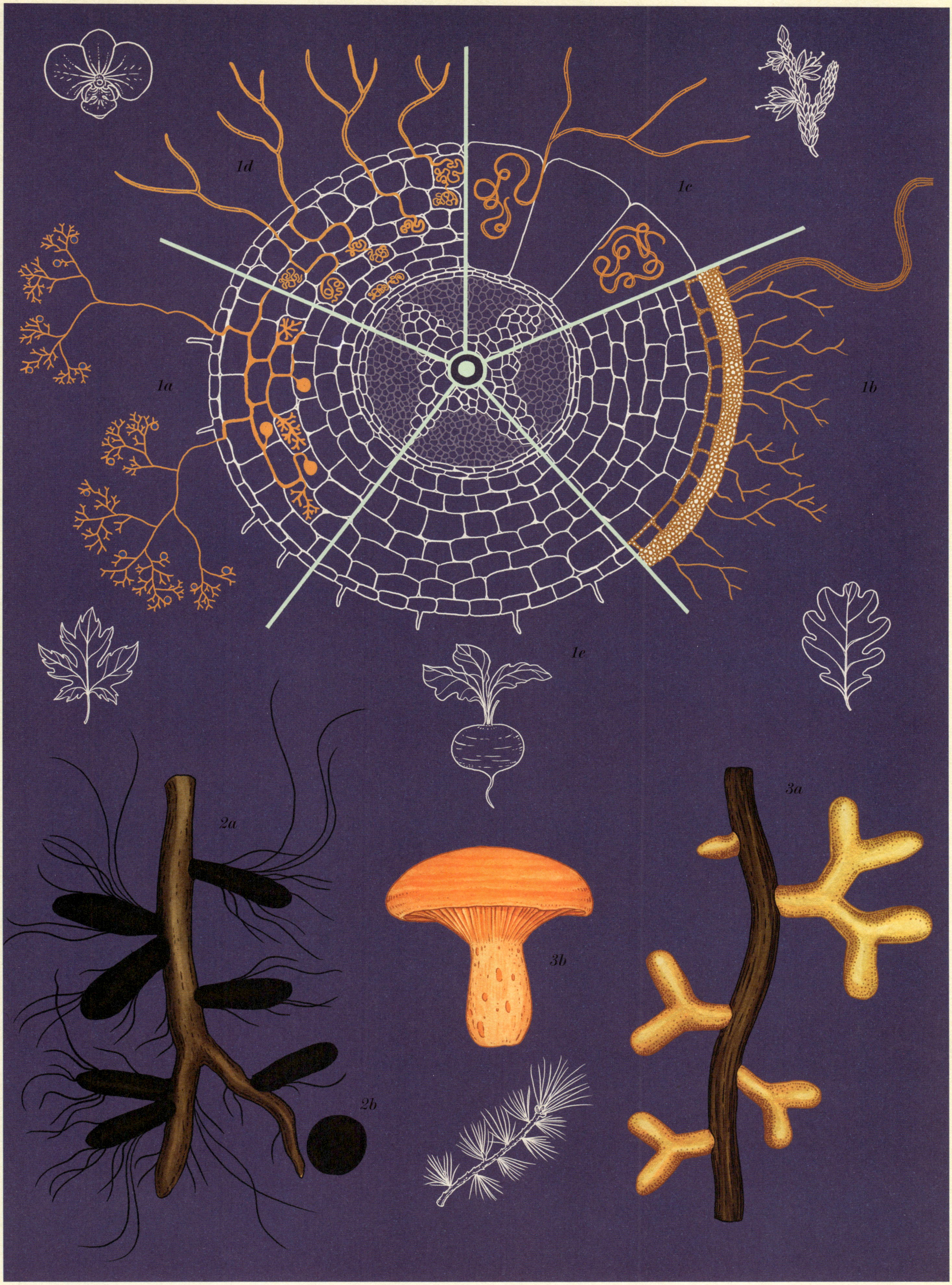

1d
1c
1a
1b
1e
2a
2b
3a
3b

Mycorrhizal Networks

Mycorrhizal fungi are connected to the roots of their host plants, forming mycorrhizas. These extend into the soil through their fungal filaments. One fungus can be attached to the roots of many plants (of the same or different species), and one plant can be attached to many different fungi. A tree can harbor dozens of fungi in its roots. In this way, fungi connect plants to one another below ground through their roots, forming the "wood wide web."

The interconnected filaments that the fungi form can be as vast and complex as forests. Sometimes we see evidence of them above ground in the form of mushrooms or crusts and below ground in the form of truffles. These are just the tip of the iceberg; the sporing bodies of the huge underground functional part of these fungi. These form extraordinarily complex communication systems known as mycorrhizal networks. In fact, a gram of soil can contain hundreds and hundreds of these fungal filaments.

Each fine root of an oak tree, as in many other trees in temperate and boreal ecosystems, is fully sheathed by a fungus that forms an ectomycorrhizal structure. These allow the mycorrhizal network to take shape. From the ectomycorrhizas, fungal filaments extend deep into the soil, gathering nutrients and water. These are transferred to trees in exchange for plant carbohydrates that the fungi use for their own growth and to form sporing bodies.

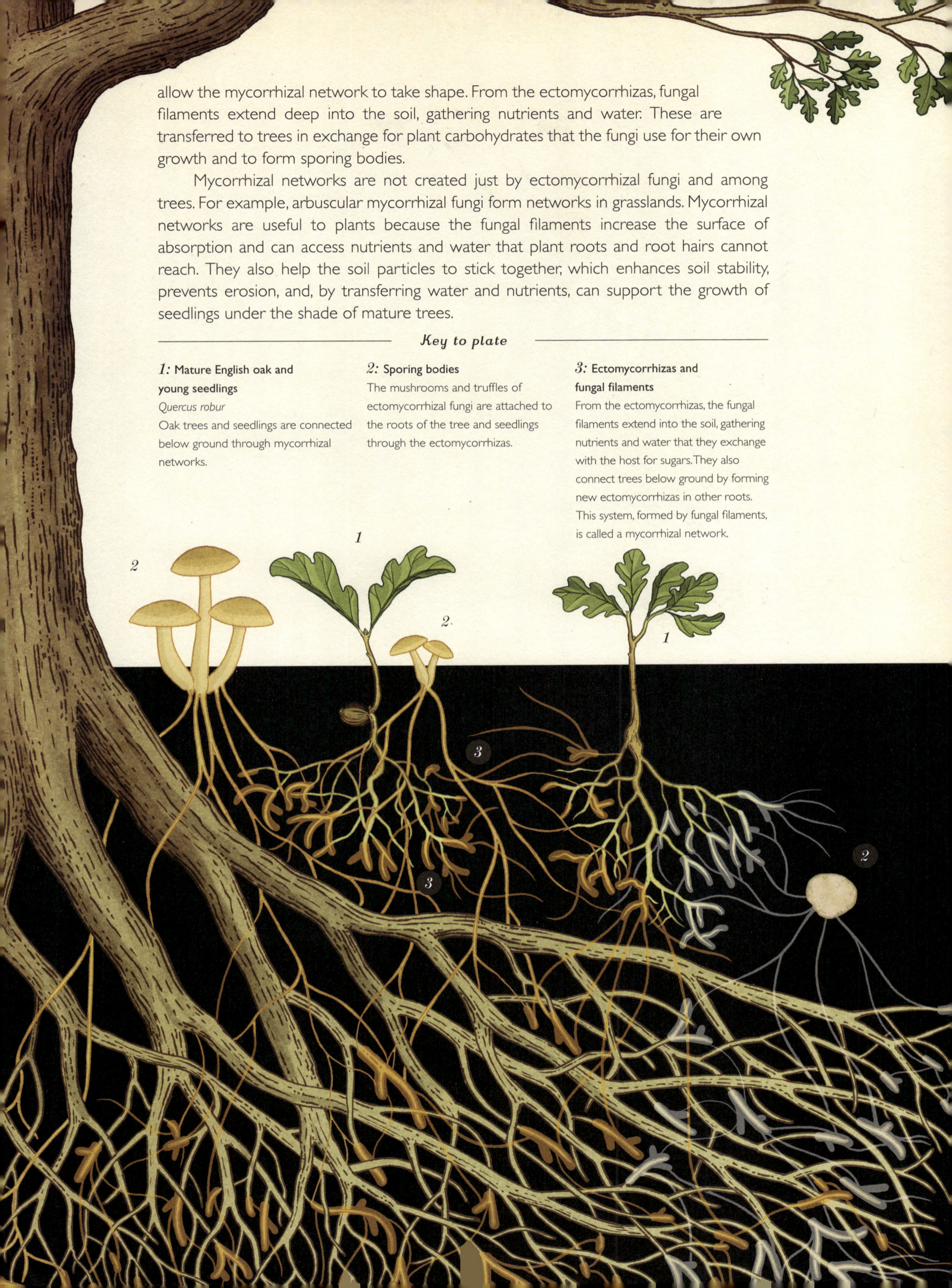

Mycorrhizal networks are not created just by ectomycorrhizal fungi and among trees. For example, arbuscular mycorrhizal fungi form networks in grasslands. Mycorrhizal networks are useful to plants because the fungal filaments increase the surface of absorption and can access nutrients and water that plant roots and root hairs cannot reach. They also help the soil particles to stick together, which enhances soil stability, prevents erosion, and, by transferring water and nutrients, can support the growth of seedlings under the shade of mature trees.

Key to plate

1: **Mature English oak and young seedlings**
Quercus robur
Oak trees and seedlings are connected below ground through mycorrhizal networks.

2: **Sporing bodies**
The mushrooms and truffles of ectomycorrhizal fungi are attached to the roots of the tree and seedlings through the ectomycorrhizas.

3: **Ectomycorrhizas and fungal filaments**
From the ectomycorrhizas, the fungal filaments extend into the soil, gathering nutrients and water that they exchange with the host for sugars. They also connect trees below ground by forming new ectomycorrhizas in other roots. This system, formed by fungal filaments, is called a mycorrhizal network.

FUNGAL INTERACTIONS

Lichens

Lichens are the result of highly successful mutualistic relationships between fungi (mycobionts) and at least one other photosynthesizing organism (photobiont), which can be an alga, a cyanobacterium, or both. The fungus benefits from the sugars produced by the photobiont, and the photobiont benefits from a place to live, physical protection, and better access to mineral nutrients. In fact, lichens are so well integrated that they were historically studied as one single species. Today, we know that nearly one-fifth of all known fungal species form lichens. More than 98 percent of those belong to the largest fungal phylum, Ascomycota, with a few species classified within Basidiomycota.

Lichens come in a huge array of shapes and colors. They can be crusty, leafy, shrublike, or hairlike and grow on almost any surface they can find: rocks, bark, soil, and even cars! Compared to other groups, lichens grow extremely slowly (from less than a millimeter to a few centimeters a year), but they seem to be extremely long-lived, with research indicating they can even survive for centuries.

Lichens are found nearly everywhere on Earth, in water, in deserts, and from the poles to the tropics. The characteristics that allow them to thrive in extreme conditions are also responsible for their high sensitivity to pollution; lichens are excellent indicators of air quality. Some are used in toothpastes and others in medicine in treatments for skin diseases and respiratory conditions. Two species are found in perfumes, and others in dyes. In boreal areas, they are a major food for caribou and reindeer.

Key to plate

1: **Cora pavonia**
One of the few examples of a basidiolichen (a lichen formed by a Basidiomycota mycobiont) and of a cyanolichen (a lichen in which the photobiont is a cyanobacterium that can fix atmospheric nitrogen instead of an alga).

2: **Bull's-eye lichen**
Placopsis gelida
An example of a three-partnered symbiosis, in which the fungus associates with two photobionts: a green alga embedded in the thallus, or main fungus body, and a nitrogen-fixing cyanobacterium, found inside separate structures called cephalodia (in this case, the brown center).

3: **Shield lichen**
Parmelia sulcata
While many lichens are highly sensitive to pollution, some, like *Parmelia sulcata*, can be very tolerant of sulfur dioxide.

4: **Brown-eyed wolf lichen**
Letharia columbiana
"Brown-eyed" in this fungus's common name refers to its disk-shaped sporing bodies, or apothecia. Wolf lichens were used in the past as poisons for wolves and foxes. This species attaches to tree bark or wood.

5: **Beard lichen**
Usnea florida
A shrub-like lichen that often ends in disk-shaped sporing bodies (apothecia), as shown here. *Usnea* species contain usnic acid, a potent antibiotic and antifungal agent. *Usnea florida* is very sensitive to sulfur dioxide air pollution.

6: **Golden-eye lichen**
Teloschistes chrysophthalmus
This shrubby lichen that grows on twigs has bright-orange apothecia surrounded by spiny projections called cilia. Its color comes from its production of parietinic acid, which can destroy or inhibit growth of microorganisms.

7: **Map lichen**
Rhizocarpon geographicum
This lichen's flat black apothecia and yellow crust make a pattern resembling a map. Map lichen grows on rocks at high elevations in areas of low pollution and is used in dating rock surfaces.

8: **Tephromela atra**
A crustose species with black sporing bodies (apothecia).

9: **British soldiers' lichen**
Cladonia cristatella
Cladonia species produce two types of thalluses, or main fungus bodies: a small-lobed primary one and a secondary stalk-like structure containing algae with the spore-bearing hymenium at the tips (bright red in this case).

10: **Umbrella basidiolichen**
Lichenomphalia umbellifera
A rare example of a basidiolichen in which the mycobiont is a mushroom. The algal cells are in squamules, small scale-like lobes, at the base.

11: **Pin lichen**
Calicium viride
This species produces its spores in a loose mass on top of a stalk, giving the appearance of dressmakers' pins.

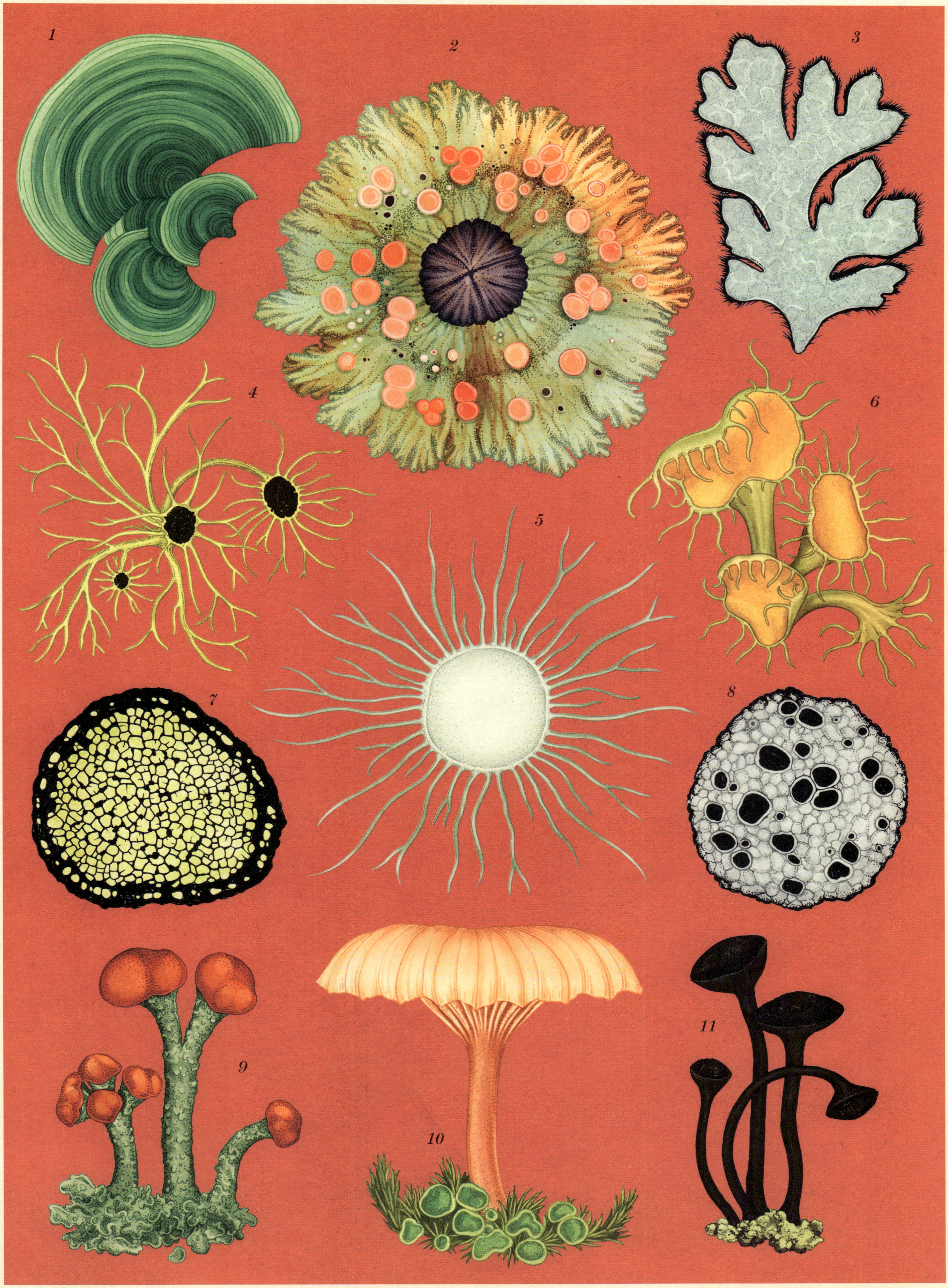
1
2
3
4
5
6
7
8
9
10
11

FUNGAL INTERACTIONS

Entomogenous Fungi

Entomogenous fungi, or entomopathogenic fungi, harm, infect, and may even kill insects. Because they occur naturally in the environment, some are used as methods for safe pest control. *Beauvaria bassiana*, for example, is used on termites, white flies, aphids, and many other species that damage plants. The spores are mixed in a solution and then sprayed on the plants that are affected.

A particular group of these fungi, most belonging to the genus *Ophiocordyceps*, has become known as "zombie fungi." They can be found worldwide in both tropical and temperate regions. It is not known how many species there are, but many infect just one type of insect. These fungi release chemicals into insects' brains and take control of their bodies. Most insects have nests below ground, but the fungus makes them find higher places in plants and trees and then bite into a leaf or branch to anchor themselves there. After this, the fungus grows rapidly in the insect's body, creating sporing bodies. The insects being situated in high spots enables the spores to spread more widely than they otherwise would.

Key to plate

1: **Dong chong xia cao**
Ophiocordyceps sinensis
This fungus infects and kills caterpillars in the Himalayan region. It is used as a traditional medicine in China and has many different applications, including as an anti-diabetic and anti-inflammatory. Over time it has become rarer and very expensive and is now endangered due to overharvesting.

2: **Weevil fungus**
Ophiocordyceps curculionum
This fungus infects weevils (*Curculionidae*), from which it gets its species name. To date, these fungi have been found only in tropical regions in South and Central America.

3: **Wasp fungus**
Ophiocordyceps humbertii
This *Ophiocordyceps* species, discovered in the Atlantic rain forest of Brazil, infects wasps. It triggers the same kind of behavior as the fungi that infect ants, such as *Ophiocordyceps unilateralis* and *Pandora formicae*. The wasp lands on a branch or leaf and bites into the fungus, which then quickly grows out to produce sporing bodies.

4: **Ant fungus**
Pandora formicae
This species only infects wood ants and is found in large parts of Europe. When the fungus makes the ants sick, they walk away from the colony. Scientists are debating if the fungus is controlling the ants or if the ants are leaving their colony to protect it.

5: **Zombie ant fungus**
Ophiocordyceps unilateralis
This fungus releases chemicals into the brain of the ant, forcing it to walk up to a high branch. The fungus grows in the body of the ant, and its spores are dispersed widely.

6: **Caterpillar fungus**
Cordyceps militaris
This fungus is found on caterpillars throughout the Northern Hemisphere.

7: **White muscardine disease**
Beauveria bassiana
Found worldwide growing naturally in the soil, this fungus infects insects and other arthropods, giving them a white fluffy look. It is used as an insecticide to control insects such as termites, aphids, and beetles.

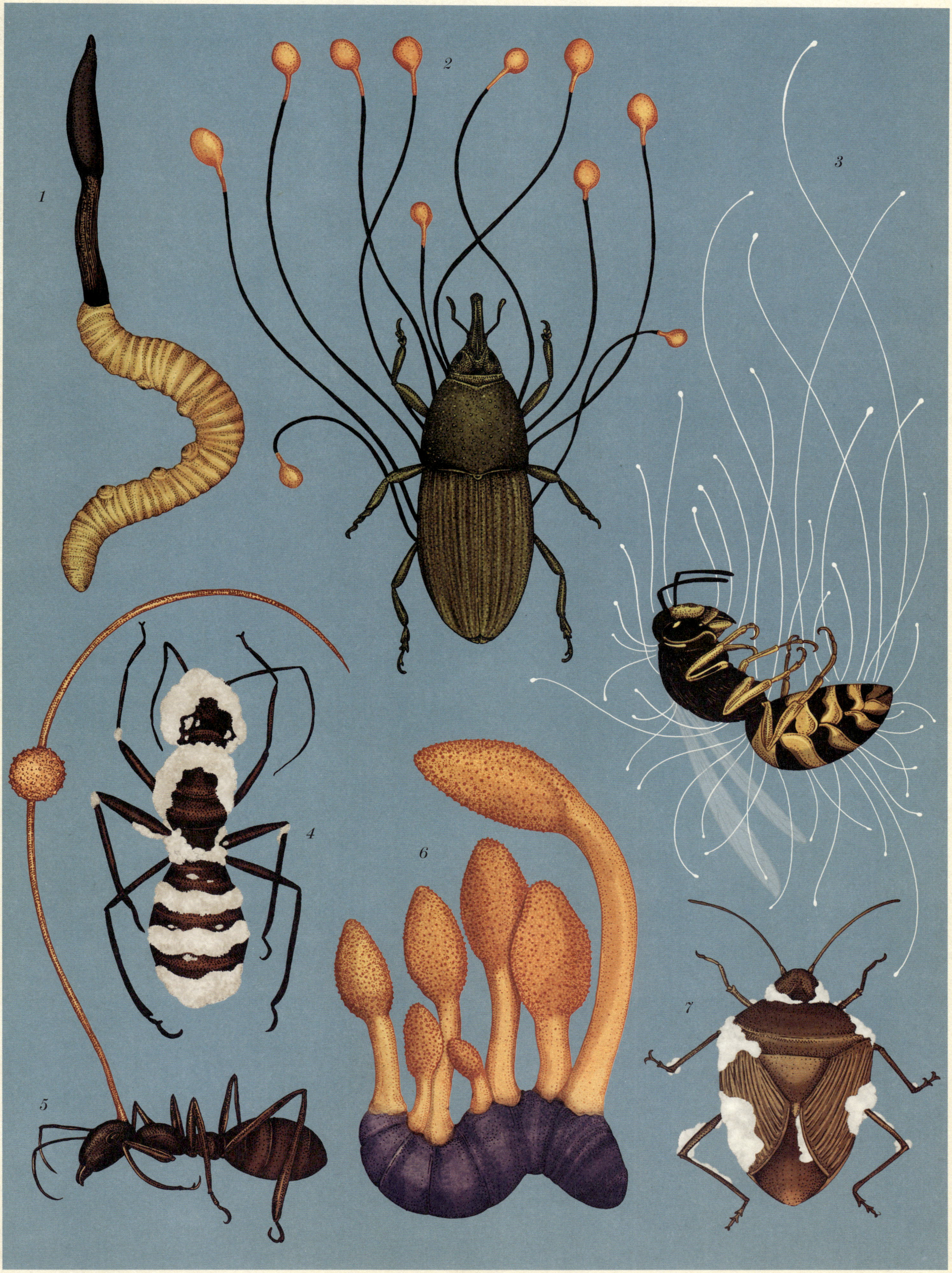
1
2
3
4
5
6
7

FUNGAL INTERACTIONS

Ants and Termites

The oldest farmers in the world are not humans, but ants and termites. While humans started growing their own food around 10,000 years ago, some species of ants and termites have been farming fungi for millions of years. These insects evolved separately from each other to cultivate their fungus food. Ants were the first farmers. Some 60 million years ago, they were growing fungus in the Amazon rain forest of South America. Termites began around 30 million years ago in the tropical forests of Africa.

Even though both ants and termites grow a fungus for food, they do so in different ways. Every year at the same time that the termites build new nests, the *Termitomyces* fungus produces mushrooms on the termites' old nests. When they crawl out of their new nests, the termites collect spores released by the mushrooms and use them to regrow their fungus gardens. Scientists call this process horizontal transfer.

Ants bring their fungus with them when they move to new nests. When a new ant queen leaves her old nest, she takes a little bit of fungus with her. The queens have a pouch inside their mouth, called the infrabuccal pocket, in which they can safely keep the fungus until their next nest is completed. Scientists call this process vertical transfer.

Both ants and termites provide food for the fungus to grow on. Leaf-cutting ants can be found walking in long lines through the rain forest with thousands of individuals carrying pieces of leaves that they have collected from trees and other plants. When they get back to their nest, they chew the leaves into little balls for the fungus to grow on. In contrast, the termites dig long underground tunnels through which they carry dead grass and plant material. After they eat this material, the fungus grows from their dung.

Key to plate

1: **Termite mushroom**
Termitomyces striatus
These mushrooms grow from the fungus that the termites cultivate. Every season, the termites collect the spores released by the mushrooms in their old nests to build new fungus gardens. *Termitomyces* mushrooms are also a delicacy for humans.

2: **Ant mushroom**
Leucoagaricus gongylophorus
Mushrooms from the ant fungus are a rare sight. They often appear when the ant colony is not doing very well. The ants do not like the mushrooms and try to remove them when they grow. It takes a lot of energy to make mushrooms, which are grown only to produce spores. Because the ants bring a piece of the fungus to build their new nests, spores are not needed. Mushrooms are therefore a waste of energy for the ants.

3: **Ant food**
Leucoagaricus gongylophorus
The fungus that the ants cultivate grows nutritious structures. These hyphal tips, called gongylidia, are swollen and packed with sugars and fats to feed the ants.

4: **Fungus-growing termite**
Macrotermes natalensis
Termites have big heads with strong jaws to protect themselves. You can find these termites throughout Africa and in Southeast Asia.

5: **Leaf-cutting ant**
Atta cephalotes
Leaf-cutting ants use their big, strong jaws (called mandibles) to cut the leaves on which their fungus grows. They also use their jaws to protect themselves from predators.

6: **Termite mound**
Macrotermes natalensis
Termites are incredible architects. They build a big mound on top of their nest. With the chimneys in the mound, the termites can control the temperature, humidity, and oxygen levels. The queen of the termites can be found safely in the middle of the nest in the "royal chamber."

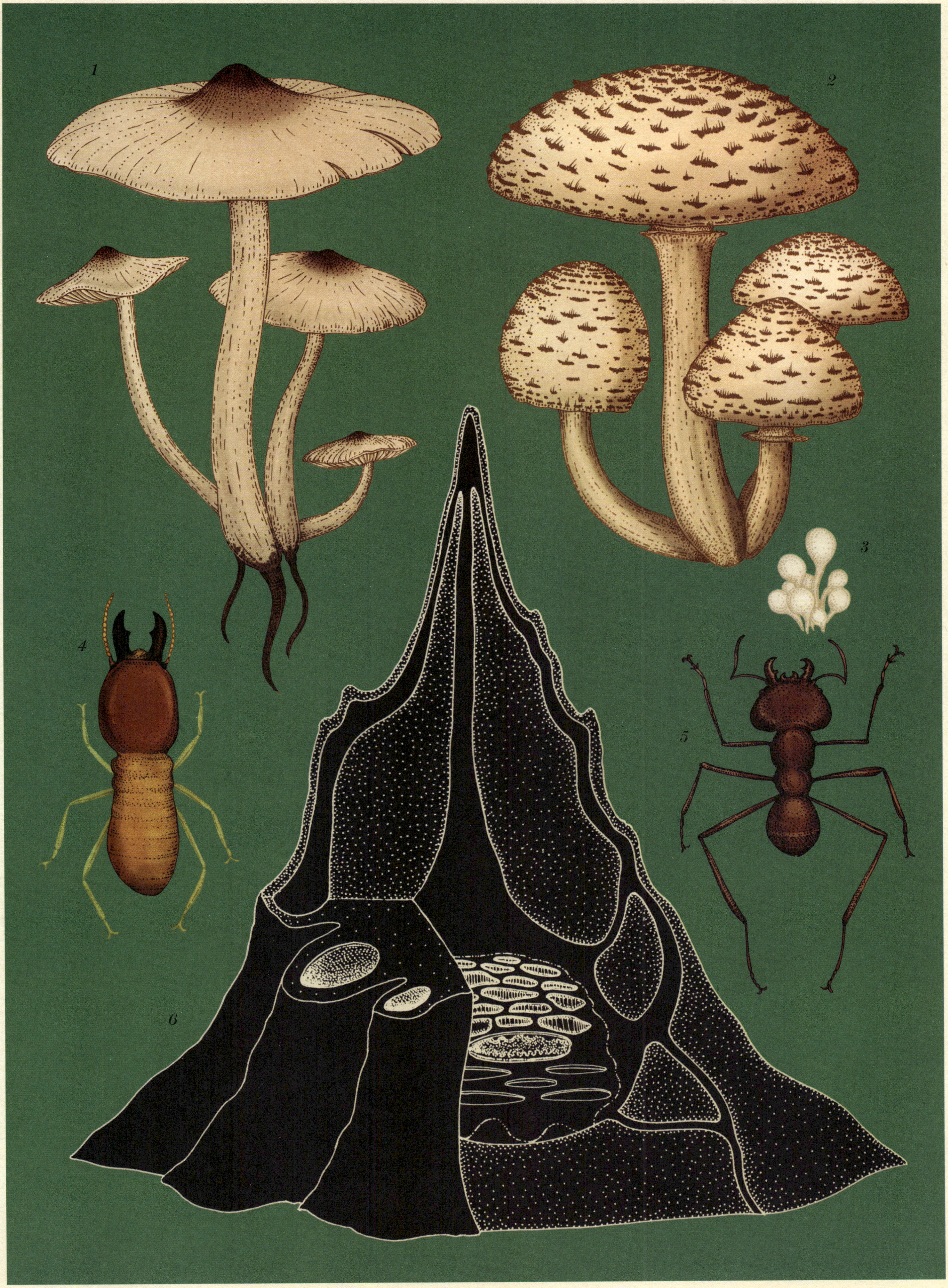
1
2
3
4
5
6

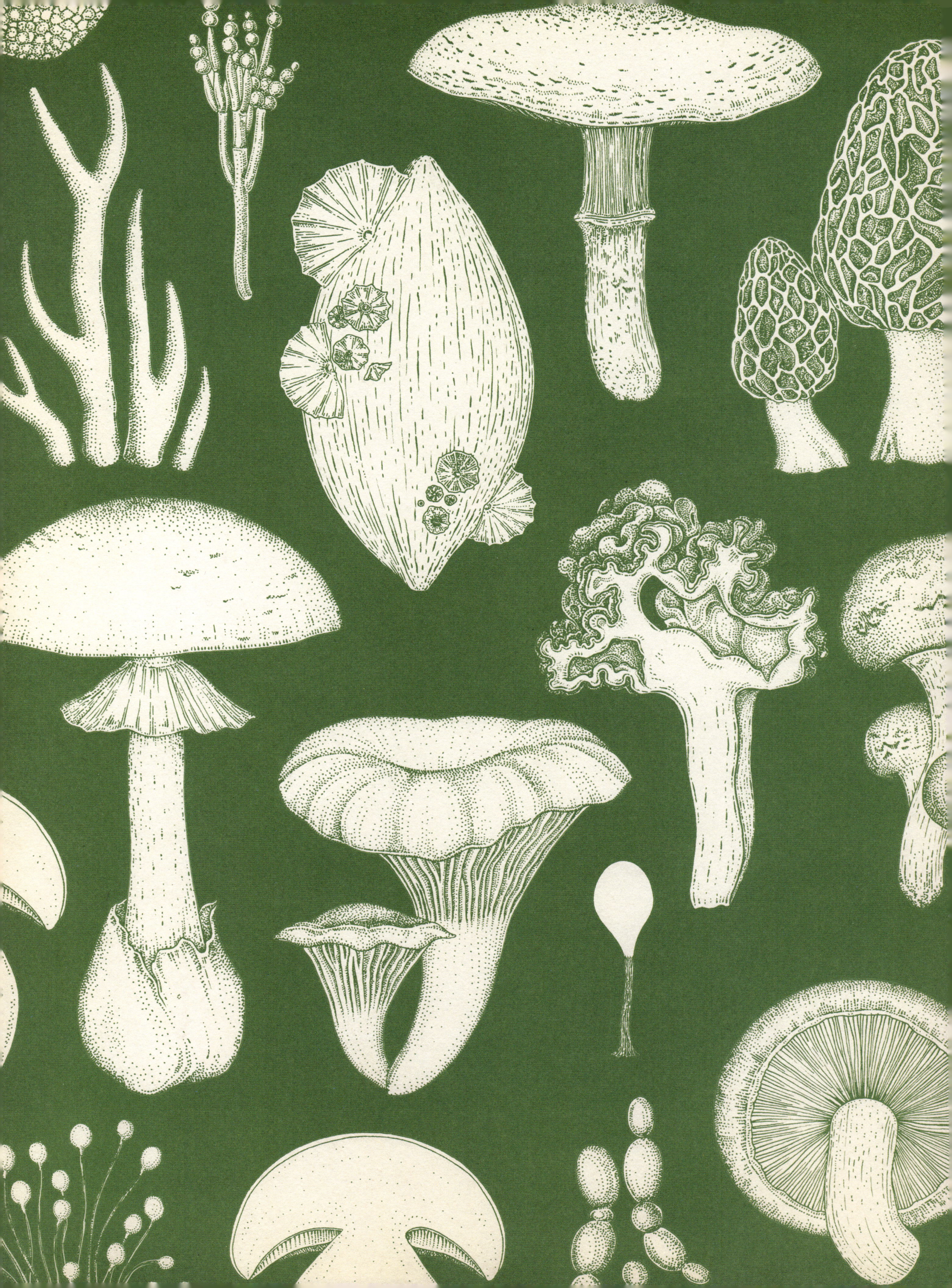

FUNGARIUM

Gallery 4

Fungi and Humans

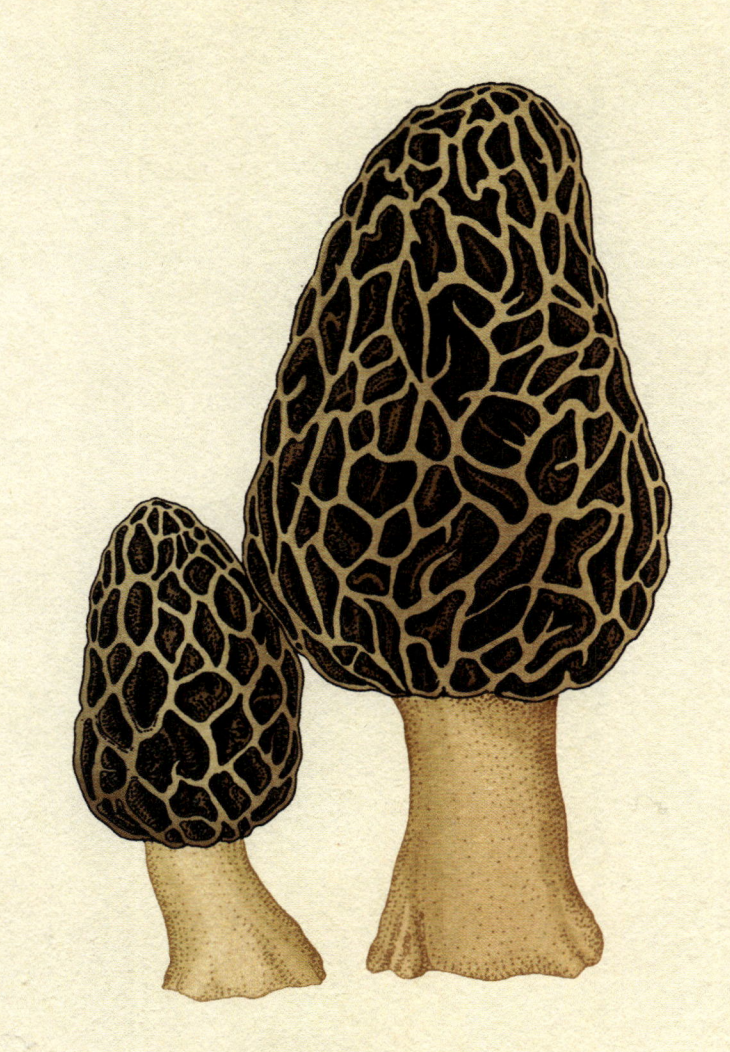

Early Mycologists
Plant Pathogens
Poisonous Fungi
Edible Fungi
Wonder Drugs
Ecosystem: Tropical Forests

FUNGI AND HUMANS

Early Mycologists

The road to understanding the fungal kingdom has been long and arduous. In classical times, it was believed that lightning strikes produced mushrooms, and even into the mid-eighteenth century, naturalists didn't understand fungi well. There were, however, small breakthroughs that began the process of defining fungi as mycologists understand them today.

The first person to really make progress was the Italian Pier Antonio Micheli (1679–1737), who was the first not only to describe and illustrate spores inside asci and on basidia but also to prove that spores could produce new fungi. But Micheli was too far ahead of his time, and much of his work was never published. Regardless, his legacy is still alive today in names he coined, including *Aspergillus*, *Clathrus*, *Mucor*, *Phallus*, *Polyporus*, and *Puccinia*.

Carl Linnaeus (1707–1778), the "father of modern taxonomy," actually set back the study of fungi rather than advanced it. His confusion around fungi led him to include them within the plant kingdom, and he grouped very different types of fungi under the same generic names.

Early mycologists also investigated organisms such as downy mildews and slime molds that we now know are not true fungi but are still named as such. For example, Reverend Miles Joseph Berkeley (1803–1889), who was the founder of British mycology and whose fungal collection began the Fungarium at London's Kew Gardens, shot to fame for his investigations into the potato blight that led to the Great Famine in Ireland (1845–1849). Berkeley confirmed that the cause was the organism we now know as *Phytophthora infestans*, a downy mildew. Arthur Lister (1830–1908) and his daughter Gulielma (1860–1949) spent decades carefully observing and illustrating slime molds, producing three editions of an exquisitely and lavishly illustrated book, *Monograph of the Mycetozoa*. Since these early observations, our understanding of the fungal kingdom has continued to evolve, and now we have a better idea of what exactly a fungus is.

Key to plate

1: **Potato blight**
Phytophthora infestans
(a) Leaves and (b) potato affected by symptoms
(c) Sporangia with sporangiophores
We now know that this and other so-called downy mildews are in fact algae that lack the chloroplasts (organelles where photosynthesis takes place) characteristic of plants. They were thought to be fungi as they can form filaments and spores similar to those of true fungi.

2: **Slime molds**
Slime molds do not share a common ancestor and belong mostly to a group called Amoebozoa.
(a) *Physarum polycephalum* in plasmodium stage: a single-celled branched network structure that seeks out food and absorbs it. Even without a nervous system, these single-celled organisms seem to communicate collectively and learn about the substances they find. They form quickly when conditions are humid.

(b) *Physarum* sporing structures
When conditions get dry, the plasmodium turns into spore-bearing structures.
(c) *Comatricha typhoides*
(d) *Comatricha nigra*
(e) *Leocarpus fragilis*
(f) *Dictyostelium discoideum*
This mold grows well in culture in laboratory conditions and is used in genetics research.
(g) *Hemitrichia calyculata*
Showing three stages of development

1a 1b 1c

2a

2c 2c 2f 2f
2b 2d 2e 2g 2g

FUNGI AND HUMANS

Plant Pathogens

Although most fungi perform helpful roles in recycling nutrients in ecosystems, some are harmful to the plants they interact with. Fungi that attack plants are called fungal plant pathogens and are a major cause of crop damage, resulting in huge financial costs in agriculture and even threatening the supply of food to our tables. The price we pay for common food items is dependent on our success in our ongoing struggle with these fungi. It is estimated that 8–21 percent of the six major food crops are lost to fungal pathogens and a further 10 percent is lost after the crops are harvested.

New plant pathogens emerge on a regular basis, but our knowledge of their existence extends back to antiquity. A student of Aristotle, Theophrastus, provided one of the first written descriptions of fungal rust diseases. In the seventeenth century in Europe, farmers observed a connection between the presence of barberry plants growing on the margins of wheat fields and the levels of stem rust damage to wheat. This proved to be a valuable insight as barberry is now known to act as a host for the wheat stem rust *Puccinia graminis*. Digging up and destroying the barberry plants turned out to be an effective way to control the rust disease.

Fungi adopt three broad strategies to infecting plants: Biotrophs live off the plants' nutrients while keeping the plants alive. Necrotrophs kill plants outright and digest the dead plant matter. And some fungi start out as biotrophs but then switch to a necrotrophic process later. Infection begins when a fungal spore lands on a plant. Next, filaments called hyphae emerge from the spore and spread across the surface of the plant, seeking a way in. Some fungi such as the rusts search out natural openings, such as the stomatal pores that allow water in and out of a plant's leaves. Others use a hardened hyphal tip to push through the leaf surface. Once they have gained entry, fungal pathogens interfere with the plant s ability to defend itself. Biotrophic fungal pathogens keep infected tissue alive despite the plant's efforts to stop the infection, while necrotrophic pathogens may release toxins to kill plant cells and then digest them.

Key to plate

1: **Basal stem rot**
Ganoderma orbiforme
This fungus causes basal stem rot in oil palm plantations in Southeast Asia. The fungus produces woody brackets on the side of the infected tree.

2: **Dutch elm disease**
Ophiostoma novo-ulmi
This fungus is a particularly aggressive cause of Dutch elm disease. It is spread by a bark beetle that lives inside the bark of the trees.

3: **Witches' broom disease**
Moniliophthora perniciosa
This pathogen infects cocoa trees, causing reduction in yield of up to 90 percent. It is resistant to fungicides.

4: **Rice blast disease**
Pyricularia oryzae
This fungus infects rice plants, causing brownish lesions to appear on the leaves. It destroys enough rice a year to feed 60 million people.

5: **Dark honey fungus**
Armillaria ostoyae
Some honey fungi are major pathogens of trees and shrubs, forming black strands called rhizomorphs, which spread through the soil and split the bark from the wood. One colony of *Armillaria gallica* forms the "humongous fungus," which occupies 3½ square miles/9.6 square kilometers in Oregon and is believed to be the largest organism on Earth.

1

4 2 3

5

FUNGI AND HUMANS

Poisonous Fungi

Despite their reputation, few fungi are dangerously poisonous. Worldwide, only about 120 species out of 22,000 mushroom-producing species are poisonous and of real concern, a mere 0.5 percent. Another 90 species can cause stomach upsets in some people, and some 150 have hallucinogenic properties. In addition, there are some molds that produce highly toxic compounds, including a *Fusarium* that has the potential to be used in biological warfare. Some of the mushrooms of most concern are common in temperate regions and have close relatives that are edible but look very similar and even belong to the same genus. Most instances of poisoning occur when a toxic mushroom is mistaken for its edible cousin, and great care must be taken when collecting mushrooms to eat. This mistake can cause nausea and vomiting or even a painful death. In Europe, however, many instances of poisoning are in dogs that have eaten *Inocybe* species, notably *Inocybe geophylla* found on lawns.

In the case of *Amanita phalloides*, the toxins attack the liver and symptoms may not appear for a day or so after it is eaten. Equally unpleasant are the toxins in some orange species of webcaps (especially *Cortinarius orellanus*); the effects of the orellanine toxin can take over two weeks to appear and cause kidney failure requiring a transplant to avoid death.

Particularly interesting is the effect of the substance ergotamine, produced by *Claviceps* species, especially *Claviceps purpurea*, which appears in curved blackish sword-like structures that sprout from the ears of cereals and other grasses. Ergotamine interferes with the nervous system, causing hallucinations, itching, and burning sensations; it also constricts blood vessels, which can result in gangrene.

Fungi have evolved to produce an enormous range of chemical products, some of which are not toxic but highly beneficial to humans, including cyclosporin, penicillins, and statins. In most cases, the role of these chemical products in nature is obscure, but it seems most likely that many serve to deter attacking insects or act as antibiotics, inhibiting the growth of bacteria and parasitic microfungi.

Key to plate

1: **Satan's bolete**
Rubroboletus satanas
(a) Exterior view
(b) Interior view
Named for its vibrant red stem and toxic nature. Even consuming very small quantities of this fungus can lead to vomiting and dehydration. When cut or bruised, the flesh turns blue.

2: **Kaentake**
Trichoderma cornu-damae
This fatal species is found in parts of Asia and is considered one of the most toxic fungi in the world. Its distinctive red sporing bodies look similar to deer antlers.

3: **Ergot fungus**
Claviceps purpurea
(a) Magnified view of sporing body
(b) Ergots seen on rye
Ergot poisoning is one of the oldest known examples of fungal poisoning, with records going back to at least 600 BCE. In Europe in the thirteenth to fourteenth centuries, when rye grass was a staple crop used in bread, poisonings often affected whole communities. Ergot's hallucinogenic properties may have been behind the behaviors that led to the 1692 Salem witch trials and executions.

4: **Destroying angel**
Amanita virosa
This deadly mushroom is found in woodlands throughout Europe and is evident in the summer and autumn months. Its sporing body is pure white.

5: **Death cap**
Amanita phalloides
Among the toxins involved in this deadly poisonous mushroom is an amanitin, which interrupts the most fundamental workings of cells by inhibiting a key enzyme, leading to cell death. This feature is being researched for its potential to attack cancer cells.

6: **False morel**
Gyromitra esculenta
The toxic false morel is named for its close resemblance to the edible true morel.

1a *1b*

2

3b

3a

4 *5* *6*

FUNGI AND HUMANS

Edible Fungi

Humans have a long history of eating fungi. We know that mushrooms have been a food source since at least the Stone Age, but they were presumably eaten earlier. In ancient Rome, Caesar's mushroom (*Amanita caesarea*) was a delicacy of emperors, and in Sweden porcini (*Boletus edulis*) is known as Karl Johan's mushroom after King Karl XIV Johan, because he taught his people to enjoy this tasty food.

The reasons we eat certain mushroom species are often based on our cultures and traditions. For example, Europe can be divided into a mainly mycophobic (mushroom-fearing) western area, where fungi are often seen as possibly poisonous, and a mycophilic, (mushroom-loving) eastern and Mediterranean area, where more species are eaten. Several peppery milkcaps (*Lactarius* spp.), for example, are commonly eaten in the eastern parts of Europe and Spain but are otherwise considered nonedible in the west.

Over the centuries, we have learned by trial and error which fungi are edible. Occasionally a new understanding might come when studying fungi using modern scientific methods. The ugly milkcap (*Lactarius turpis*) was once considered an edible mushroom but is today known to contain a compound that causes genetic mutations.

The global market for edible mushrooms is worth about $42 billion a year and includes both wild and cultivated mushrooms. Almost all cultivated species, such as button mushrooms (*Agaricus bisporus*), are decomposers, since they can be easily grown in dead organic matter. However, many of the most flavorsome gourmet mushroom species, like porcini, are mycorrhizal, which means that they live in a relationship with plants and are very hard to cultivate. There are some exceptions such as the black truffle, which grows underground and can be cultivated with oak trees (*Quercus*).

Globally at least 350 species of fungi are collected for food. The most commonly collected wild mushrooms are brittlegills (*Russula*), milkcaps (*Lactarius*), boletes (*Boletus*), agarics (*Amanita*), and chanterelles (*Cantharellus*).

Wild mushroom gatherers must be careful, however, since some edible mushrooms can cause allergic reactions in some individuals. Some mushrooms that are safe to eat also resemble poisonous species. It is also unsafe to collect food from polluted areas, since heavy metals in soil can accumulate in mushrooms.

Key to plate

1: **Matsuke**
Tricholoma matsutake
Matsuke can be found in coniferous forests in Asia, Europe, and North America. It is highly valued in Japan, where it has been eaten for thousands of years.

2: **Button mushroom**
Agaricus bisporus
These are generally cultivated but are native to grasslands, especially in North America.

3: **Chanterelle**
Cantharellus cibarius
Chanterelle mushrooms are native to Europe. They are one of the easiest edible species to recognize.

4: **Black truffle**
Tuber melanosporum
The black truffle of southern Europe is one of the more expensive edible species in the world.

5: **Caesar's mushroom**
Amanita caesarea
Caesar's mushroom grows in southern Europe and North Africa.

6: **True morel**
Morchella esculenta
The true morel is common in Europe. It looks somewhat similar to the poisonous false morel, *Gyromitra esculenta*.

7: **Baker's yeast**
Saccharomyces cerevisiae
Baker's yeast was probably first isolated from the skins of grapes.

8: **Penicillium roqueforti**
This fungus is a constituent of blue cheeses, known to have been eaten by humans since 50 CE.

9: **Zeller's bolete**
Xerocomellus zelleri
This edible bolete is found in western North America.

10: **Cabbage lungwort**
Lobaria linita
Several species of this lichen genus are used in soups and as medicines.

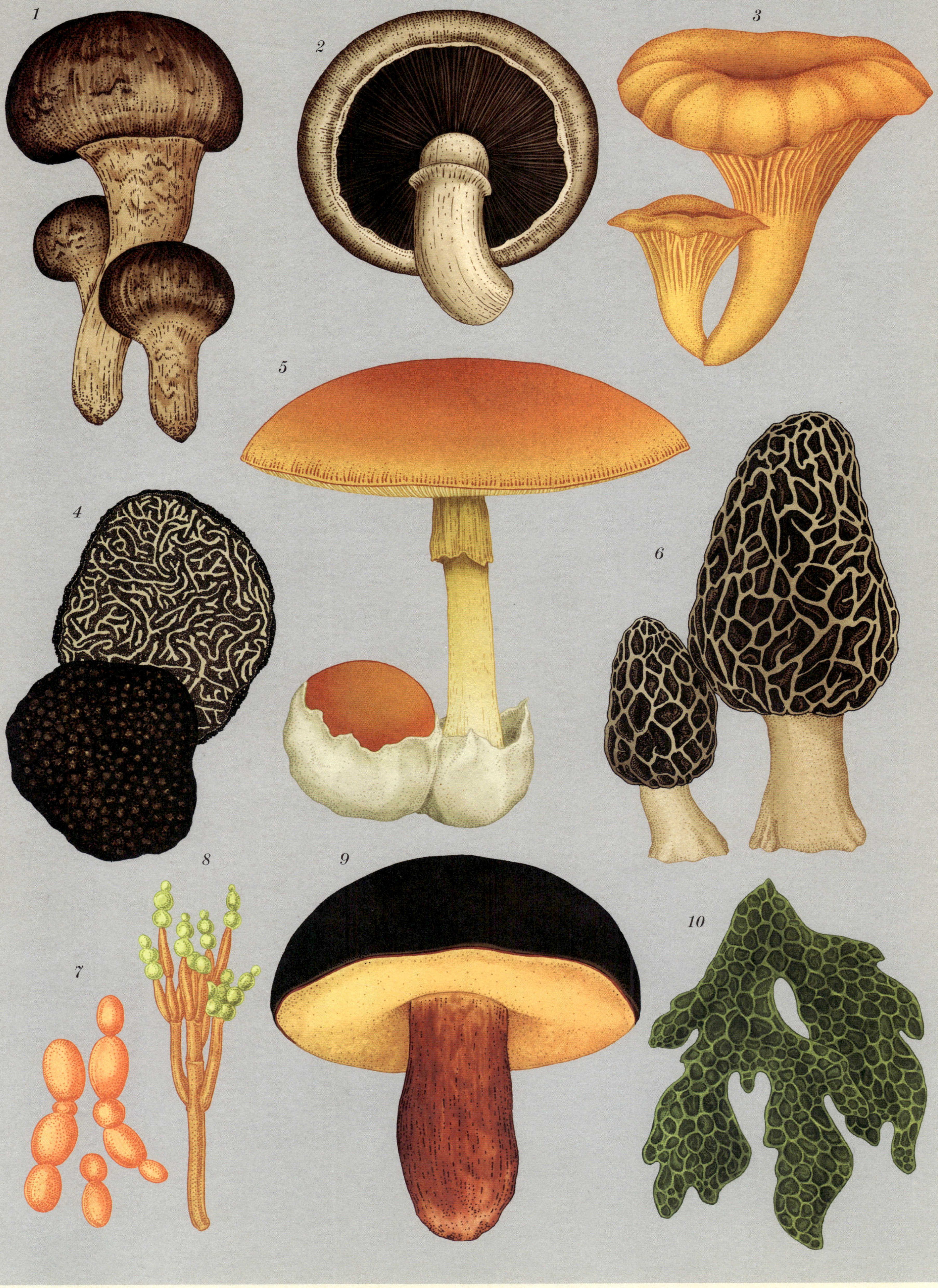
1
2
3
4
5
6
7
8
9
10

FUNGI AND HUMANS

Wonder Drugs

Fungi are the source of some of the most important medicines ever discovered. Around the world, scientists research them in the hope of finding the next lifesaving drug. The properties that make some fungi so useful in human medication may perform a useful role in the wild, for example, inhibiting the growth of competitor bacteria. Some fungi—such as, most famously, penicillin—have redefined what's possible with medicine.

The story of penicillin starts in the London laboratory of the microbiologist Alexander Fleming in the 1920s. Fleming's petri dish contained a culture of *Staphylococcus* bacteria but was also accidentally contaminated with a *Penicillium* mold. Fleming noticed that the *Staphylococcus* could not grow near the mold and wondered if it was producing some kind of inhibitory chemical. Follow-up work by Howard Florey and his team at Oxford identified the inhibitory substance as penicillin and demonstrated its incredible powers for treating bacterial infections.

The realization that infection could be treated so effectively with a chemical from a fungus stimulated a worldwide hunt for fungi that produced other useful substances. One antibiotic discovered as a result was cephalosporin C, produced by *Acremonium chrysogenum*, which was isolated from a sewage outlet. A more recent discovery is the antifungal drug caspofungin, which comes from a chemical in *Glarea lozoyensis*.

Fungi have also proved to be a fantastic source of immunosuppressants—drugs that lower the response of the human immune system. Two important immunosuppressant compounds, cyclosporine and myriocin, come from fungi that grow inside insect larvae. These suppress the animals immune systems but keep them alive as a source of nutrients. Cyclosporine made organ transplantation possible by preventing the immune system from rejecting the transplanted organ, while myriocin has been altered to produce a highly effective treatment for multiple sclerosis.

There are also the statin drugs, whose founding member, lovastatin, was isolated from the mold *Aspergillus terreus*. The discovery of lovastatin has helped stimulate the development of the wider statin class, which inhibits cholesterol synthesis and reduces the likelihood of cardiovascular disease. Discoveries such as this raise the obvious question: Where will be the next fungal wonder drug be found?

Key to plate

1: Glarea lozoyensis
Colony growing on culture plate
This fungus was isolated from streams in the mountains of central Spain.

2: Penicillium rubens
(a) Colonies of *Penicillium rubens* growing on a culture plate
(b) Appearance under light microscope

3: Tolypocladium inflatum
The fungus is able to infect scarab beetles and produces the immunosuppressant compound cyclosporine, which is thought to help it evade the beetle's immune system. Cyclosporine can also suppress the human immune system and has revolutionized the field of organ transplantation. Previously, transplantations were generally unsuccessful as the organ was rejected by the recipient's immune system.

4: Aspergillus terreus
(a) Colony growing on culture plate
(b) Appearance under light microscope
Aside from its effects in humans, lovastatin has antifungal properties, suggesting its role in nature may involve deterring competitor fungi.

5: Isaria sinclairii
Infected cicada nymph
This fungus produces the immunosuppressant compound myriocin. Like cyclosporine, myriocin is thought to help the fungus evade its host's immune system. Myriocin inspired the creation of a synthetic derivative called fingolimod, which is a highly effective new treatment for the autoimmune disease multiple sclerosis.

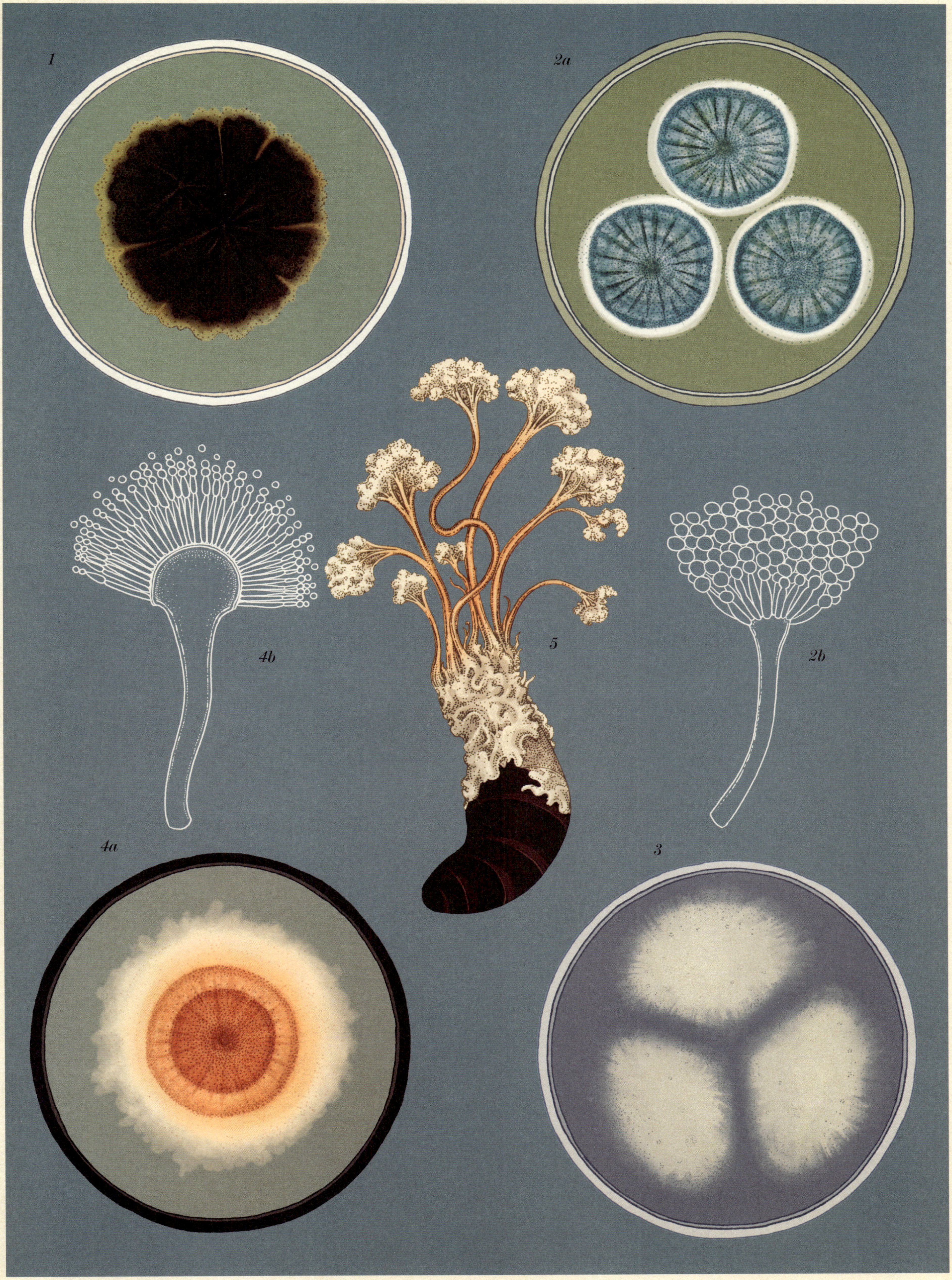
1
2a
4b
5
2b
4a
3

FUNGI AND HUMANS

Ecosystem: Tropical Forests

Step into a tropical rain forest and the first thing you notice (apart from the busy noise of insects) is its lush, diverse vegetation, with a myriad of leaf shapes and tree heights. The trees grow extremely densely, with about 150–200 species per 2½ acres/1 hectare, compared to just 5–10 in temperate forests. Green all year round, rain forests don't have marked seasons, so there is no autumnal flush of mushrooms. Instead, fungi are seen sporadically throughout the year.

In contrast to boreal and temperate forests (pages 18 and 32), where the trees are almost always ectomycorrhizal (pages 36–39), those in tropical forests tend to associate with fewer species of endomycorrhizal fungi. This does not mean that tropical forests are species-poor in fungi. Scientists estimate that there are likely to be six to seven times as many fungi as plants growing in any one area. So the tropics, with many more plants than temperate regions, are an amazing source of unexplored fungal diversity.

Leaves of many tropical trees live for several years and develop a patchwork of specialized microscopic fungi, including lichen-forming species. Huge tree trunks can be covered by mosaics of shade-loving crustose lichens that live partly within the bark. Meanwhile, the vast quantities of wood and leaf litter that fall to the forest floor are broken down by fungi. One of the most visible forest floor fungi in the tropics are the brightly colored *Cookeina* species.

Tropical forests are enormously rich in insects, particularly beetles, some of which have minute fungi sticking out from their exoskeletons like tiny brushes, while their guts have been found to contain numerous yeasts that are new to science.

Key to plate

1: Pleurotus djamor
This bracket fungus is saprotrophic, meaning it breaks down organic matter.

2: Letrouitia domingensis

3: Deflexula subsimplex
An example of coral fungus. This highly modified mushroom is shaped like worms and grows on trunks.

4: Christmas wreath lichen
Herpothallon rubrocinctum
This crust lichen grows on tree bark in shaded, moist forests in tropical and subtropical areas. Its common name is inspired by its concentric red and green bands.

5: Spotted cort
Cortinarius iodes
An ectomycorrhizal fungus that produces mushrooms with slimy purple caps and yellowish spots.

6: Amethyst deceiver
Laccaria amethystina
This mycorrhizal species can also be found in temperate regions.

7: Indigo milkcap
Lactarius indigo
As with all members of this genus, *Lactarius indigo* produces latex, or milk, when the mushroom is cut or broken. In this case, the latex is indigo blue.

8: Golden-scruffy collybia
Cyptotrama asprata
Appearing in all tropical regions, this saprotrophic fungus lives on branches and sticks.

9: Cobalt crust
Terana coerulea
The cobalt crust fungus appears as beautiful blue crusts on dead branches.

10: Pycnoporus sanguineus
This bracket fungus is mostly found on dead wood in the Southern Hemisphere.

11: Pod parachute
Gymnopus montagnei

12: Cookeina speciosa
(see also page 22)

13: Lactocollybia aurantiaca

14: Marasmius haematocephalus

15: Parrot waxcap
Gliophorus psittacinus

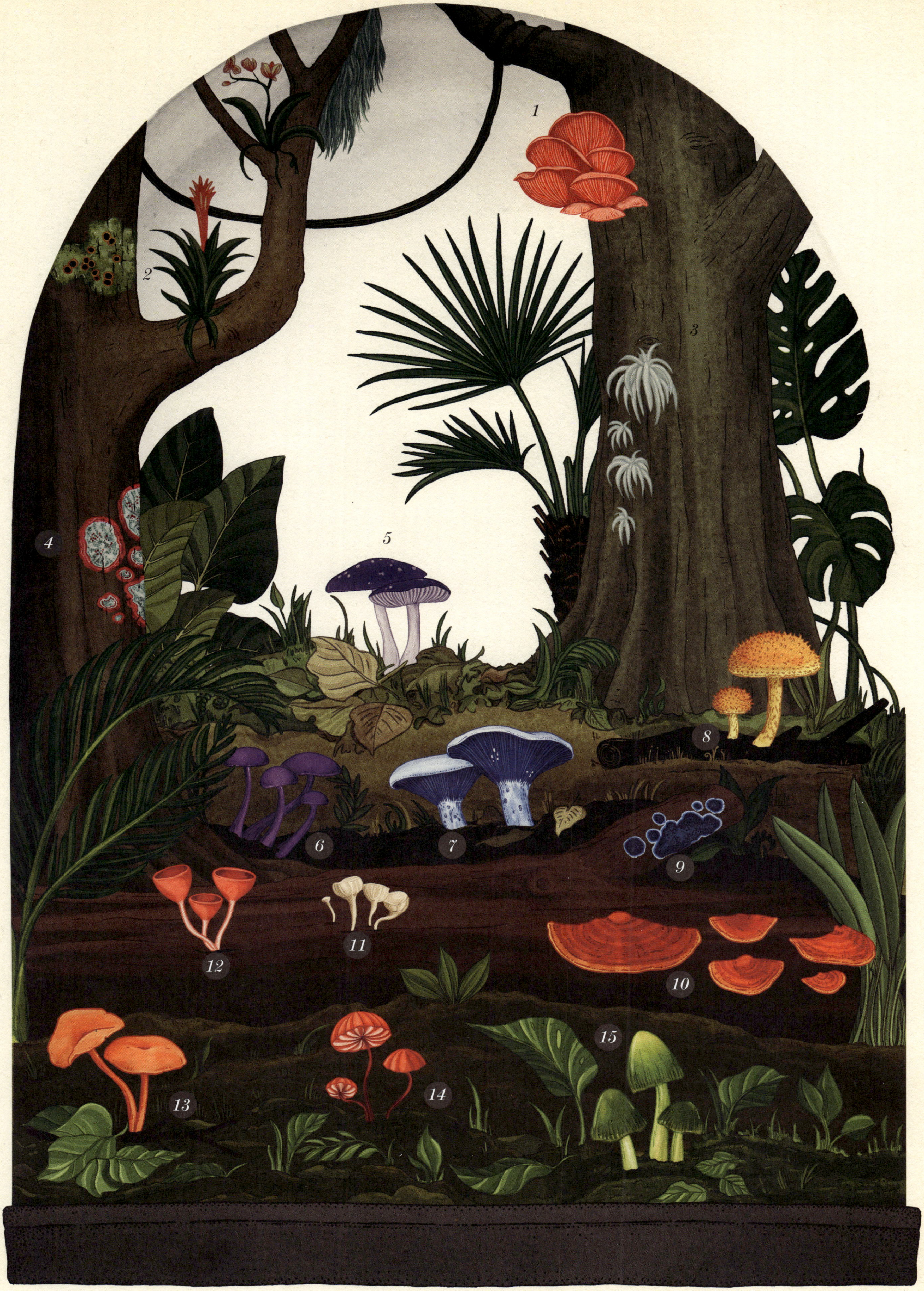
1
2
3
4
5
6
7
8
9
10
11
12
13
14
15

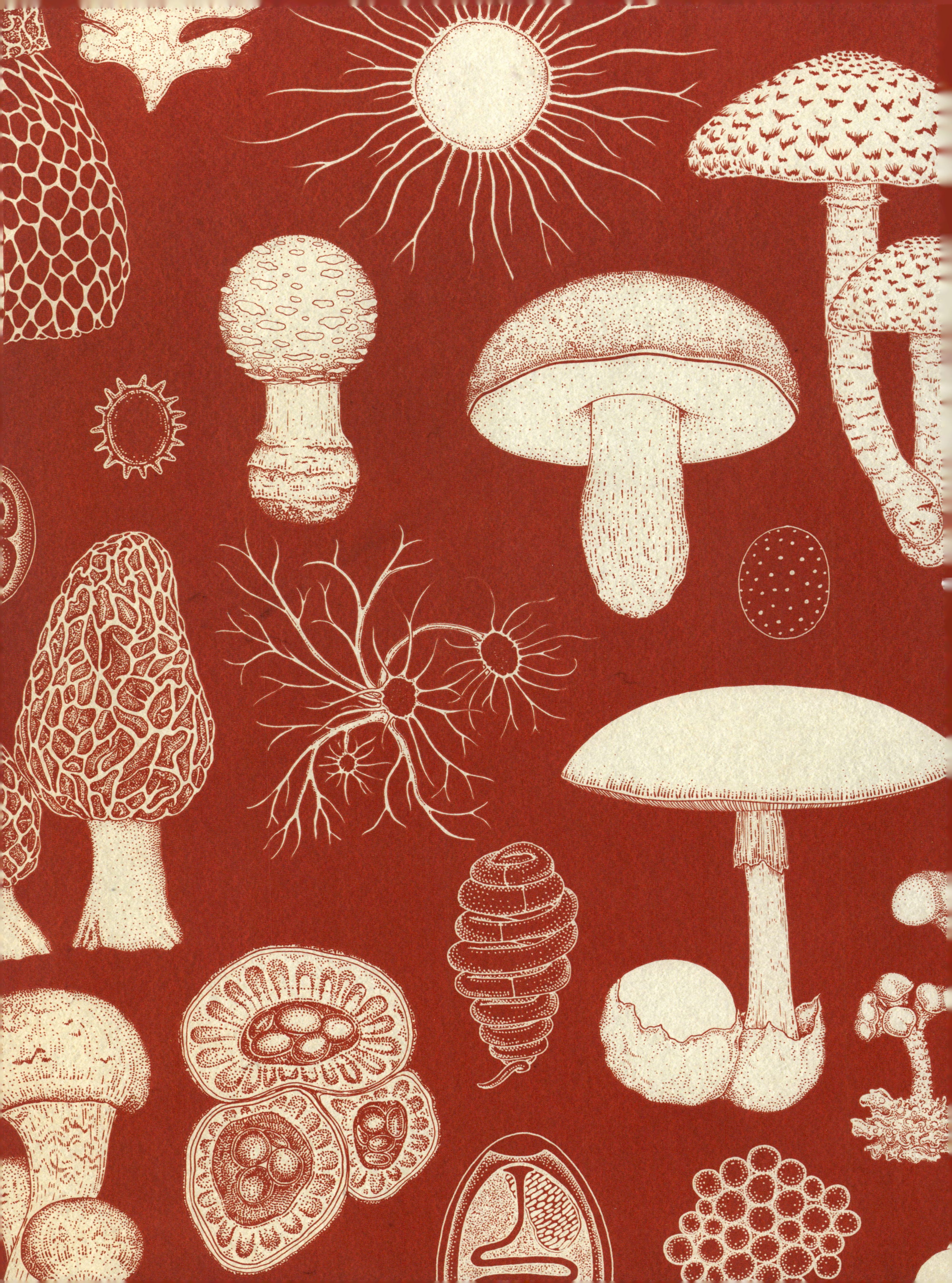

FUNGARIUM

Library

Index
Curators
To Learn More

Index

Acremonium chrysogenum 56
agarics 54
Agaricus bisporus 54
Agaricus campestris 10
Aleuria aurantia 22
algae 8, 26, 30, 32, 40, 48
alpine brittlegill 18
alpine webcap 18
alpine zone 18
Alternaria alternata 12
Alternaria sesami 15
Amanita caesarea 8, 54
Amanita muscaria 24
Amanita phalloides 52
Amanita virosa 52
amethyst deceiver 58
Anguillospora longissima 15
ant fungus 42, 44
antibiotics 52, 56
ants 42, 44
arbuscular mycorrhizas 36, 39
Armillaria ostoyae 50
asci 8, 10, 30, 48
Ascomycota 3, 5, 10, 40
Aspergillus terreus 56
Atta cephalotes 44

baker's yeast 54
basal stem rot 50
Basidiomycota 3, 10, 26, 40
beard lichen 40
Beauvaria bassiana 42
beech trees 8, 32, 36
beech milkcap 32
beefsteak fungus 26, 32
Berkeley, Miles Joseph, Rev. 48
Berwaldia schaefernai 8
biotrophs 50
bird's-nest fungus 28
black bread mold 8
black earth tongue 22
Blastocladiomycota 2, 5, 8
blue mold rot fungus 16
blue roundhead 24
boletes 18, 32, 52, 54
Boletus edulis 54
bracket fungi 26
British soldiers' lichen 40
brittlegills 18, 54
brown-eyed wolf lichen 40
Buglossoporus quercinus 26
bull's-eye lichen 40
button mushrooms 54

cabbage lungwort 54
Caesar's mushroom 8, 54
Calenia monospora 15
Calicium viride 40
Calocera sp. 18
Calocera viscosa 18
Caloscypha fulgens 22
Calvatia sculpta 28
candlestick/candle-snuff fungus 10
Cantharellus cibarius 54
Caryospora callicarpa 15
caterpillar fungus 42
Cenococcum geophilum 36
chaga 26
chanterelles 32, 36, 54
chemicals 42, 52, 56
chicken of the woods 32
chitin 5, 8
Chlorociboria aeruginosa 22
Christmas wreath lichen 58
Chytridiomycota 2, 5, 8
Cladia aggregata lichen 8
Cladonia cristatella 40
Claviceps purpurea 52
clustered bonnet 32
cobalt crust 58
Coemansia erecta 12
Colus hirudinosus 28
Comatricha nigra 48
Comatricha typhoides 48
commensals 5
conidia 12, 30
Cookeina speciosa 22, 58
Coprinus comatus 24
Cora pavonia 40
Cordyceps militaris 42
Cornutispora lichenicola 15
Corollospora lacera 14
corticioid fungi 26
Cortinarius alpinus 18
Cortinarius bibulus 24
Cortinarius iodes 58
Cortinarius orellanus 52
Cortinarius traganus 18
Cortinarius violaceus 24
Craterellus tubaeformis 32
crust fungi 26, 58
Cryptomycota 2, 5, 8
cup fungi 22
cyanobacteria 32, 40
Cyathus striatus 28
Cyptotrama asprata 58
Cyttaria darwinii 8

Dacrymyces stillatus 10
Darwin's fungus 8
death cap 52
deceivers 18, 58
Deflexula subsimplex 58
destroying angel 52
Dictyostelium discoideum 48
dog lichen 10
dong chong xia cao 42
downy mildews 5, 48
drugs 52, 56
Dutch elm disease 50

earthball 28, 32
earthstars 28
ecosystems 18, 26, 32, 36, 38, 58
ectomycorrhizas 18, 32, 36–39, 58
edible fungi 24, 28, 32, 54
Entoloma sp. 18
entomogenous fungi 42
environmental conditions 32
ergot fungus 52
ergotamine 52
ericoid mycorrhizas 36
Evernia prunastri 32
evolution 5
eyelash fungus 22

fairy rings 24
false morel 52
Favre's fiber cap 18
fiber caps 18
field mushrooms 10
Fistulina hepatica 26, 32
flagellum 5, 8
Fleming, Alexander 56
Florey, Howard 56
fly agaric 24
foliicolous fungi 30
Fomes fomentarius 26
forests 18, 32, 38, 58
fungicolous fungi 30
Fusarium 52

Ganoderma orbiforme 50
gassy webcap 18
gasteromycetes 28
Geastrum quadrifidum 28
Geastrum saccatum 28
Gelasinospora micropertusa 15
giant elm bracket 26
gills 10, 24, 26, 28
Glarea lozoyensis 56

gleba 28
Gliophorus psittacinus 58
golden-eye lichen 40
golden-scruffy collybia 58
green elf cup 22
growth 16
Gymnopus fusipes 32
Gymnopus montagnei 58
Gymnopus perforans 18
Gyromitra esculenta 52

hare's ear 22
Harknessia spermatoidea 14
Hebeloma sp. 18
Helicomyces scandens 14
Helicoon ellipticum 15
Hemitrichia calyculata 48
Herpothallon rubrocinctum 58
honey fungus 50
Hygrocybe sp. 24
hyphae 8, 10, 12, 16, 30

immunosuppressants 56
indigo milkcap 58
Inocybe favrei 18
Inocybe geophylla 52
Inonotus obliquus 26
insects 42, 44, 58
Isaria sinclairii 56
isidia 12

jelly fungi 18
jellyspot fungus 10

kaentake 52
Kew Gardens. *See* Royal Botanic Gardens, Kew

Laccaria amethystina 58
Laccaria sp. 18
Lactarius blennius 32
Lactarius deliciosus 36
Lactarius indigo 58
Lactarius quietus 32
Lactarius sp. 18, 54
Lactarius turpis 54
Lactocollybia aurantiaca 58
Laetiporus sulphureus 32
Lasiodiplodia theobromae 12
leaf-cutting ant 44
leaves 30, 58
Leccinum versipelle 18
Leocarpus fragilis 48

Letharia columbiana 40
Letrouitia domingensis 58
Leucoagaricus gongylophorus 44
lichenometry 16
Lichenomphalia umbellifera 40
Lichenopeltella palustris 30
lichens
   growth 16
   human uses 40, 54
   reproduction 10, 12
   temperate forests 32
   tropical forests 58
   types 8, 22, 30, 40
Linnaeus, Carl 8, 48
Lister, Arthur 48
Lister, Gulielma 48
Lobaria linita 54
Lobaria pulmonaria 32
Lophotrichus ampullus 14
Lycoperdon perlatum 28

Macrotermes natalensis 44
map lichen 40
Marasmius haematocephalus 58
Marasmius oreades 24
matsuke 54
matte bolete 32
Meliola urariae 30
Micheli, Pier Antonio 48
Microsporidia 2, 5, 8
mildews 5, 48
milkcaps 18, 32, 36, 54, 58
Moniliophthora perniciosa 50
Morchella esculenta 54
morels 54
mountains 18
Mucor sp. 16
Mucoromycota 3, 5, 8, 10
mushrooms 10, 24, 26, 28, 54
mycelium 16, 24, 30
Mycena inclinata 32
mycobionts 40
mycologists 48
mycorrhizas 22, 26, 36–39
Myxomycota 5

necrotrophs 50
Neonectria ditissima 15
Neurospora lineolata 15

oak trees 32, 36, 38–39, 54
oak milkcap 32
oak polypore 26
oakmoss lichen 32
Oomycota 5
Ophiocordyceps curculionum 42
Ophiocordyceps humbertii 42
Ophiocordyceps sinensis 42
Ophiocordyceps unilateralis 42
Ophiostoma novo-ulmi 50
orange birch bolete 18

orange peel fungus 22
orchid mycorrhizas 36
organelles 16, 48
Otidea onotica 22
Ötzi the Iceman 26

Pandora formicae 42
parasites 5, 8
Parenglerula macowanianus 30
Parmelia sulcata 40
Parmelina pastillifera 12
parrot waxcap 58
pathogens 5, 12, 16, 26, 50
Peltigera canina 10
Peltistroma juruanum 30
penicillins 52, 56
Penicillium baarnense 15
Penicillium expansum 16
Penicillium roqueforti 54
Penicillium rubens 56
Periconia byssoides 12
Pertusaria pertusa 15
Pestalotiopsis guepinii 15
Phallus indusiatus 28
Pholiota squarrosa 24
photobionts 40
Phragmidium violaceum 10
phyla 8
Physarum polycephalum 48
Phytophthora infestans 48
pin lichen 40
pin molds 16
pinkgills 18
Piromyces communis 8
Placopsis gelida 40
Plectania chilensis 22
Pleurotus djamor 58
pod parachute 58
Podoscypha multizonata 32
Podospora fimiseda 15
poisonous fungi 24, 52
poison pies 18
polypores 26
porcini 36, 54
potato blight 48
propagules 15
Puccinia graminis 50
puffballs 28
Pycnoporus sanguineus 58
Pyricularia oryzae 50

Quercus robur 38–39, 54

Ramaria sp. 32
Ramaria stricta 8
reproduction 10, 12
Rhizocarpon geographicum 40
rhizomorphs 16
Rhizophydium planktonicum 8
Rhizopus stolonifer 8
rice blast disease 50

Rigidoporus ulmarius 26
Rinodina confragosula 15
rounded earthstar 28
Royal Botanic Gardens, Kew 26, 48
Rozella sp. 8
Rubroboletus satanas 52
Russula nana 18
Russula sp. 18, 54
Russula viridofusca 15
rust diseases 50
rust fungus 10

Saccharomyces cerevisiae 54
saffron milkcap 36
saprobes/saprotrophs 12, 24, 28, 32, 58
Sarcoscypha austriaca 22
Satan's bolete 52
scalycaps 24
scarlet elf cap 22
Schizoxylon ligustri 15
Scleroderma citrinum 28, 32
sclerotia 32, 36
sculpted puffball 28
Scutellinia scutellata 22
Sebacina sp. 18
shaggy ink cap 24
shaggy scalycap 24
shield fungus 30
shield lichen 40
slime molds 5, 48
slimy milkcap 32
soralia 12
spindle toughshank 32
spores 8, 10, 12, 14–15, 22, 28, 30
Sporormiella leporina 15
spotted cort 58
spring orange peel fungus 22
Stachybotrys chartarum 16
statins 56
sterigmata 10
stinkhorns 28
stinking parachute 18
Strigula orbicularis 30
Stropharia caerulea 24
Suillus granulatus 18
symbiosis 18, 30, 32, 40

Teloschistes chrysophthalmus 40
temperate forests 22, 32
Tephromela atra 40
Terana coerulea 58
termites 42, 44
Termitomyces striatus 44
Termitomyces titanicus 24
Tetrachaetum elegans 14
Tetracladium sp. 12
Theophrastus 50
Thielaviopsis basicola 12
tinder fungus 26
toadstools 24

Tolypocladium inflatum 56
Tomentella sp. 18
toxic black mold 16
tree lungwort 32
trees 18, 26, 32, 36, 38–39, 50, 58
Triangularia bambusae 15
Tricharia urceolata 30
Trichoderma cornu-damae 52
Trichoderma viride 16
Trichoglossum hirsutum 22
Tricholoma matsutake 54
tropical forests 58
tropical lichen 30
truffles 15, 36, 38, 54
trumpet chanterelle 32
Tuber melanosporum 54

ugly milkcap 54
umbrella basidiolichen 40
upright coral 8
Usnea florida 40
Ustilago koenigiae 15

veiled lady 28
violet webcap 24

wasp fungus 42
waxcaps 24, 58
webcaps 18, 24, 52
weeping bolete 18
weevil fungus 42
white muscardine disease 42
witches' broom disease 50
wolf lichens 40
wood decayers 16, 26, 32
"wood wide web" 38–39

Xerocomus badius 15
Xerocomellus pruinatus 32
Xerocomellus zelleri 54
Xylaria hypoxylon 10

yeasts 5, 12, 16, 54
yellow stagshorn 18
yellowfoot 32

Zeller's bolete 54
zombie ant fungus 42
zombie fungi 42
zoned rosette 32
Zoopagomycota 3, 5, 8
zoospores 3–4, 5, 8
Zygopleurage zygospora 15
Zygorhynchus sp. 10

Curators

Katie Scott is illustrator of *Animalium* and *Botanicum*, which were also produced in collaboration with the Royal Botanic Gardens, Kew. *Animalium* was chosen as the *Sunday Times* (London) Children's Book of the Year. Katie studied illustration at the University of Brighton and is inspired by the elaborate paintings of Ernst Haeckel.

Ester Gaya is a senior research leader at Kew. She began her career in mycology in Spain and after some time in the United States decided to settle in England. She has spent the past twenty years researching fungi. She is especially fascinated by lichens and tries to understand their evolution.

David L. Hawksworth CBE has wide pure and applied mycological interests. He was the last director of the International Mycological Institute and is an honorary president of the International Mycological Association and an honorary research associate of the Royal Botanic Gardens, Kew.

Laura M. Suz is a research leader in mycology at Kew. She has spent almost twenty years digging up tree roots and looking at their ectomycorrhizas. Laura did her PhD in Spain on edible truffles. She moved to London in 2010 to investigate the fungi that associate with oak and the threats to their diversity.

Pepijn W. Kooij has studied fungus-farming ants for almost ten years in the hot tropics of Panama. Born in the Netherlands, he spent his visits to the zoo looking at leaf-cutting ants. He did his PhD in Denmark. In 2015, he moved to London to prove that it is not fungus-farming ants, but rather ants-farming fungi.

Kare Liimatainen is a Finnish mycologist with a PhD from the University of Helsinki who has also worked in Sweden and the United States. Working with colleagues, he has found dozens of new fungal species in the UK over the last four years. His happiest memories are of trips to North America, where the seasons were perfect and he was surrounded by masses of beautiful fungi.

Tom Prescott is a research leader at Kew. His work focuses on investigating the natural chemicals found in plants and fungi, with a special focus on their effects on human cells and the model fungal organism *Saccharomyces cerevisiae*. He also travels to Papua New Guinea to research the medicinal plants used there.

Lee Davies comes from a paleontology and invertebrate fossil background. After a stopover working on tropical African plants, he has become Kew's mycology curator. He lives nomadically in London, on a narrowboat.

To Learn More

Mycological Societies
British Lichen Society
www.britishlichensociety.org.uk

British Mycological Society
www.britmycolsoc.org.uk

Fungus Conservation Trust
www.abfg.org

International Association for Lichenology
www.lichenology.org

International Mycological Association
www.ima-mycology.org

The Fifth Kingdom
An online version of Bryce Kendrick's popular mycology textbook, with over 800 pictures and animations.
http://mycolog.com/fifthtoc.html

Species Fungorum
Coordinated by Kew, this initiative gives current names for fungal species. If you come across an unfamiliar name, this is the must-go-to site.
www.speciesfungorum.org

Royal Botanic Gardens, Kew
Learn about Kew's global and collaborative scientific work, making an invaluable contribution to solving some of the biggest environmental challenges facing humanity. Kew houses the world's largest fungarium with over 1.25 million dried specimens from all over the world.
www.kew.org
www.kew.org/science/collections-and-resources/collections/fungarium

State of the World's Fungi (2018)
Prepared by international scientists and published by Kew, this resource gives numerous facts on many topics included in *Fungarium*.
https://stateoftheworldsfungi.org

US National Fungus Collections
Database of collections held by the US Department of Agriculture, including collections previously held by the Smithsonian Institution.
https://data.nal.usda.gov/dataset/us-national-fungus-collections

Westerdijk Fungal Biodiversity Institute Utrecht, the Netherlands
This institute maintains around 100,000 cultures of fungi and hosts the MycoBank database owned by the International Mycological Association.
www.westerdijkinstitute.nl
www.mycobank.org